JERKY

Other Cookbooks by A. D. Livingston

Sausage
Cold-Smoking Sausage
Cold-Smoking & Salt-Curing Meat, Fish, & Game
Cast-Iron Cooking
The Whole Grain Cookbook
Venison Cookbook
The Curmudgeon's Book of Skillet Cooking
Complete Fish & Game Cookbook
Freshwater Fish Cookbook

JERKY

MAKE YOUR OWN DELICIOUS JERKY AND JERKY DISHES USING BEEF, VENISON, FISH, OR FOWL

A. D. LIVINGSTON

LYONS PRESS
Guilford, Connecticut
An imprint of Globe Pequot Press

Lyons Press is an imprint of Globe Pequot Press.

The author would like to thank the friends, guests, and cooks who
have contributed to this book. Specific acknowledgments to indi-
viduals, other books, and authors are made in the text as appropri-
ate. A few of the recipes and a little of the text were used, in slightly
altered form, in the author's column for *Gray's Sporting Journal*.

Project editor: Gregory Hyman
Layout: Kevin Mak
Text design: Elizabeth Kingsbury

Library of Congress Cataloging-in-Publication Data is available on
file.

ISBN 978-1-59921-984-4

Printed in the United States of America

10 9 8 7 6 5 4 3 2

Contents

Introduction

Jerky is simply raw meat that has been slowly dried at low temperature. As the water is removed, the meat loses both weight and volume. What it doesn't lose, however, is flavor. In fact, the flavor of the meat is greatly concentrated, which might explain why just about everybody with good teeth loves jerky.

These days jerky is popular as a snack, and it also comes in handy as a high-energy food for backpackers, dogsledders, trail walkers, hunters, anglers, boaters, and other people who spend lots of time outdoors. For long-distance runners and sports competitors, jerky can deliver a burst of energy all out of proportion to its compact size and light weight. For campers, jerky is easy to pack and store. On an auto trip, jerky is great for the kids and doesn't make a mess in the car, and, of course, it's perfect for snacking during the football game or television shows—and for sneaking into movie theaters that don't allow their patrons to bring their own popcorn. Family dogs savor the stuff, too, if my Nosher is a good representative.

Indeed, modern man eats jerky by the ton, piece by savory piece. It's available these days in supermarkets and outfitter shops and through mail-order catalogs and ".com" companies—and even in corner convenience stores. In other parts of the world, freshly made jerky is often sold at wayside stands and by street vendors. More and more people are making it at home these days, in this country and abroad, and packets of jerky seasoning mixes are sold in sausage and jerky supply catalogs and at the meat counters of large supermarkets.

These days deer hunters are perhaps America's greatest jerky makers, in terms of volume, because they sometimes have large amounts of meat to preserve and because jerky seems to be a popular chew among this group. Also, a lot of dehydrated-food buffs—many of whom have purchased expensive food dehydrators and vacuum-pack systems for home use—are especially interested in making their own jerky.

Historically, jerky making is usually attributed to the American Indian, who made good use of it to store buffalo and other meats for future use and for journey food. But jerky really wasn't first invented in the Americas. It has been made around the world since the time of the caveman, and records of its use date back as far as the ancient Egyptians. Before the invention of caning and refrigeration, drying was the only way to preserve meat.

Jerky is still a practical way of preserving meat for future use. Yet modern man, for the most part, has taken to jerky for a more epicurean reason: Jerky simply tastes good and lasts longer, as a chew, than other foods or snacks. And since jerky is made from low-fat cuts of meat, it is also healthier than most junk food.

As a practitioner, I believe that the very best jerky is made at low temperature over a long period of time. There are, however, other opinions and practical considerations in this matter. If truth be told, there's simply more than one way to jerk meat. Recipes abound and techniques vary. Experts set forth conflicting information in books and magazine articles. Practitioners argue hotly, head to head. In truth, just about every jackleg jerky maker has something to share, as well as secrets to keep, and I hope the variety of recipes and methods in this book, old and new, will prove to be interesting and helpful. These variations will be discussed in more detail in the chapters that follow, along with suitable recipes. Meanwhile, here is some information that applies to all jerky making.

The Shape of Jerky

Most jerky these days is cut into thin strips. True, some commercial jerky is made in rather jagged pieces, but most of it is made in a more uniform size. Pressed jerky, which is made from ground or chopped meat, is almost always quite uniform. The strips of meat usually run about 5 or 6 inches long by 1 inch wide, and often less than ¼ inch thick; when the strips of meat are dried, the dimensions shrink considerably. In any case, the length and width of the strips aren't nearly as important as the thickness, which greatly influences how long the jerky should be dried and how it will be eaten. Thick jerky tends to make a better chew and lasts longer, but thin requires less drying time and is easier to chew up for quick consumption.

Cutting the Meat

A sharp knife is the jerky maker's best friend. I always prefer blades made of carbon steel, because they can easily be sharpened with the aid of a good Arkansas whetstone. Modern stainless-steel knives and various sharpening devices fall into the gadget category. If you don't believe me, talk with some professional butchers who don't sell cutlery.

An electric meat saw comes in handy for making jerky, especially if you are a stickler for uniform thicknesses. There are also some other aids for cutting jerky in uniform thicknesses. Check the mail-order and Internet sources listed at the end of this book. Meanwhile, keep your knife sharp.

Almost always it's best to partly freeze the meat before attempting to slice it thinly. How thin should it be? Most practitioners want ¼ inch thick or less. Not only does the thickness help determine the time required to dry the meat, but it also has a bearing on the texture of the finished jerky. The texture is also influenced greatly by the grain of the meat and how it is cut. If the jerky is cut with the grain, lengthwise, it will be stringy and tough, which is what most people want for a good chew. If it is cut across the grain, it tends to be crumbly and easier to chew up and swallow. Jerky that will be used in pemmican or in recipes (see part 3) works best if it is cut across the grain.

When drying a batch of jerky, there is no rule stating that all your pieces must be of the same thickness or overall shape. It is, however, best to keep thick separated from thin, on separate trays. That way, you can dry the thicker strips longer without having to judge each piece in the whole batch.

This might come as a cultural shock to some people, but jerky does not have to be made in narrow strips. Chapter 4 sets forth recipes for jerky nuggets, chunks, and slabs. So . . . if you are inept at carving meat with a knife, jerk it all and enjoy the variety.

One other thing. You should wash your hands and utensils before and after cutting meat. This precaution is especially important before handling meat that is to be cut into chunks and then ground for making burger jerky.

Drying Jerky

Modern practitioners are fortunate enough to have kitchen ovens and electric dehydrators suitable for making jerky. These are convenient, yes, but good jerky has been made for centuries without them. The idea, of course, is to remove the moisture from the meat at a low temperature. The several ways to accomplish this are detailed in the chapters in part 1 of this book, including how-to texts on drying jerky in kitchen ovens, in electric dehydrators made especially for drying foods, in the open air, in patio smokers, and so on.

The weight of the finished jerky as compared to the weight of the fresh meat is a pretty good indication of dryness. For the best overall results, 5 pounds of beef should be dried down to about 2 or 2½ pounds of jerky. For long storage, however, it can go on down to about 1 pound—but this jerky will be very hard and will lose some flavor. A good deal depends on the meat, however. Some venison, for example, will be considerably drier than most beef.

Most people don't bother to weigh the meat before and after jerking it in order to determine dryness. Instead, experience usually prevails. Properly prepared jerky feels dry to the touch; strips of jerky will bend without snapping but will at the same time show cracks and breaks in the bend.

Clearly, drying jerky at home is not an exact science. There are too many variables, such as temperature, air circulation, humidity of the ambient air, drying time, thickness of the meat, and so on. The "cure" that the practitioner uses also affects the process.

The trend of minimizing salt in modern jerky recipes or techniques is not recommended by this writer—but some excellent-tasting recipes do just that. I argue that the salt is very important, partially because it stimulates the taste buds, but mainly because it helps preserve the meat directly and helps draw the moisture out. Most bacteria simply can't thrive without adequate moisture. For a more detailed discussion, see appendix A, "Jerky Ingredients and Safety."

STORING JERKY

There are several approaches to and some conflicting opinions about the best way to store jerky. Some practitioners put it into an airtight jar or other container, whereas others want to store it in a cloth bag so that it can breathe. Some people tell you to keep it in a brown bag; others say not to do so under any circumstances. Some of the recipes and methods throughout this book will reflect some of these opinions, which in turn often apply to the jerky made by a certain procedure and under certain conditions.

If I had to be pinned down to one method of storing jerky, I would wiggle a little but in the end I would surely choose wide-mouthed Mason jars sealed with the new vacuum-pack systems, now available for the home kitchen. In some cases, vacuum-packed plastic bags work better than Mason jars.

Much depends on the temperature and humidity of the air. In cool dry climates, jerky stores satisfactorily without refrigeration, and the storage method isn't very important. In hot humid climes, it's best to store the jerky in the refrigerator (which will usually be low in both humidity and temperature) or in a freezer. If the jerky is to be kept outside the refrigerator, I prefer to either vacuum-seal it or keep it in a breathable container. Often I'll wrap the strips in paper towels, which tend to wick away any moisture the jerky might contain or absorb on a humid day. Jerky wrapped a few strips at a time in paper towels and stored in a pillowcase will keep for a very long time, if it is properly dried to start with.

Sometimes jerky that wasn't quite dry enough for storage will develop a mold on the surface. This can be wiped off with a cloth dipped in vinegar, but most people find that the mold quells their appetite for that particular batch of jerky.

Keep in mind that jerky taken from an oven or a dehydrator will become harder as it cools. Also remember that such jerky will continue to dry out during storage if the humidity is low. So, air can work in two ways: Moist air will add moisture to the jerky; dry air will draw moisture out of the jerky. Using a vacuum-pack system will minimize either action simply by removing the air. Consequently, I highly recommend the vacuum-pack systems for storing jerky as well as fish and fresh meats in the refrigerator or freezer. These machines are very easy to use. Just follow the manufacturer's instructions, making sure that you have the proper kind of bags and new lid seals for the jars.

One other tip: Always allow the jerky to cool down before storing it in an airtight container. Hot jerky tends to sweat.

USING JERKY

Jerky isn't limited to snacks. It can be eaten in other ways, or cooked for a meal. Chapter 11 sets forth recipes and techniques for making and using pemmican—an American Indian mixture of powdered jerky and animal fat, which is storable and easy to eat. Chapter 12 contains some recipes for using jerky in complete one-pot dishes, such as the old cowboy Jowler and chili. Anyone who puts up lots of jerky, perhaps as a means of preserving the meat from a moose or elk taken on the hunt, may want to cook these dishes fairly often, and, of course, culinary adventurers will want a taste of the old ways of doing things.

WHY MAKE YOUR OWN JERKY?

Jerky is expensive if you buy it ready-made and neatly packaged in small units. But it's really inexpensive, or can be, if you make your own in bulk and don't go overboard on spices and herbs. At $3.00 per pound for the meat, homemade jerky will figure out at about $7.50 per pound. You'd pay that for an ounce or two of gourmet jerky ordered from a catalog. The price can be even lower if you buy and jerk a big chunk of meat, such as a beef hindquarter from a meat-processing plant or even a large roast from your favorite butcher. Put the pencil to it.

Jerky tastes better fresh than it does after long storage, and jerky is at its very best when eaten directly from the oven or dehydrator, still warm and not as hard as it will become on cooling. Trouble is, warm jerky is just a little *too* good. More than one batch (never mind whose) has been entirely consumed by the "testing" while it was still drying in the oven. Warm jerky is addictive, really, and my mouth starts to water just to think of it as I write these words. You can taste it, too. Lean back in your easy chair, close your eyes, and whiff the aroma gently wafting from the kitchen oven.

—A. D. Livingston
Wewahitchka, Florida

PART ONE

Ways to Make Jerky

The chapters in part 1 set forth several methods and a number of recipes for making jerky in the kitchen, on the patio, and in remote camps. Most of the recipes and techniques call for a lean red meat or some commonly understood cut such as flank steak. These recipes can be adapted quite readily to venison, lean beef, and other good red meats—with some emphasis on "lean." Specific meats such as beef, venison, and ostrich are discussed in part 2, along with recipes for jerking them.

1

KITCHEN OVEN JERKY

The ordinary kitchen oven permits the home cook to make excellent jerky without any specialized equipment or start-up costs. Usually, jerky strips are simply placed on the crosspieces of the oven racks, possibly with a drip pan at the bottom. A few people may prefer to hang the jerky vertically from the racks. To accomplish this, it's easy to skewer the end of each strip with a toothpick and hang it, but the process is time consuming. Multiple strips can be threaded onto bamboo skewers, properly spaced to hang between the metal rods. Draping the strips of meat directly over the metal rods isn't recommended, however—except possibly for very thin jerky—but long strips can be folded over two rods for better air circulation. Also, drying the meat on trays with a solid bottom isn't ideal, because the bottom of the jerky isn't exposed to air.

One problem with a tightly closed oven is that the moisture from the jerky can't escape and slows the drying process. Leaving the door slightly ajar helps, but will alter the temperature of the oven. It's best to check the oven temperature with a thermometer instead of relying on the thermostat.

Of course, one oven may not be quite as good as another for making jerky, and each type will have advantages or disadvantages. Here's my take:

Electric Ovens. The electric kitchen oven can be credited with bringing about the recent renaissance in homemade jerky.

As a general rule, the door should be left slightly ajar, letting the water vapor escape from the oven. Most kitchen ovens come with two racks, which can be used in several positions. Additional racks can be obtained for some models, either at retail outlets, from the manufacturer, or perhaps from flea markets and junk stores. For best results, test the temperature of your own oven with a thermometer placed in the center. Make the test after the oven has been turned on for an hour, with the door ajar. In other words, test the oven under the conditions that will be used for making jerky. If the oven thermostat is not accurate, compensation can usually be made. Also make sure that only the bottom heating element is in use. This will normally be the bake mode. The broil mode heats from the top element. Some oven preheat modes use both top and bottom. In any case, if your oven uses both the top and bottom elements for regular baking, it's best to unplug the top element before making jerky.

Auxiliary Toaster Ovens. These small ovens come in handy for making a small batch of jerky, starting with about a pound of meat. Remember that with most of these small ovens you'll have only one rack, which should be in the center position. Also remember to use the bake mode, not the broil. Put the thermostat on the lowest setting, which will usually be marked WARM. Then turn it up if needed, testing the actual temperature in the middle with an oven thermometer. Leave the door cracked open (slightly) to let the moisture escape.

Convection Ovens. Basically, these are regular ovens with fans to circulate the air. In size they range from countertop to full-size kitchen ovens, such as the Jenn-Air. Some have regular dehydrating modes, and some have a space for water vapor to escape—a very good feature for drying jerky. In general, they heat evenly and do a good job of making jerky. It's best to follow the manufacturer's instructions for these ovens. They are more expensive than

3

dehydrators, but the larger ranges are really useful appliances to have for regular cooking as well as for drying foods. They also operate as regular oven, convection oven, broiler, and dehydrator, as well as having a stovetop grill and burners on top. Moreover, some of these ovens hold up to ten racks. In any case, the manufacturers of convection ovens publish instruction books and even cookbooks, which cover dehydrating.

I don't recommend buying a convection oven for making jerky. But if you already own one, or plan to add one to your kitchen for regular cooking, then by all means take advantage of its dehydrating capability. The forced-air-circulation feature is great for drying jerky, as compared to regular ovens, but note that merely circulating the same air in the oven in a closed loop will not help remove the moisture from the system. Read the manufacturer's instructions—and remember that dry air is the key to making good jerky, always.

Gas Ovens. Most of these are not ideal for jerky simply because they get too hot. After all, the idea is to dry the meat, not cook or toast it. Before attempting a batch of jerky in a gas oven, turn the thermostat to the lowest setting and put a thermometer inside close to the center. To be suitable for jerky, it should read 150 degrees or lower. If the oven has a pilot light, try making jerky without turning on the main burner. This will usually take considerably longer, however, depending on the internal temperature, but it will make the jerky at a low temperature.

Woodstove Ovens. These old-time ovens can be used for making jerky if the temperature is held low enough. The better way would be to start the jerky in the oven for a few minutes, then hang it over the stove. The air will naturally rise from the stove, bringing heat to the jerky and taking away any water vapor. See also chapter 3.

• • •

The rest of this chapter sets forth recipes for making jerky in a large electric kitchen oven. Adjustments can be made as necessary for other types of ovens. Bear in mind that these recipes can also be used to make jerky in a dehydrator (see chapter 2). The measures of the meat in these recipes are suited for making jerky on two large racks. For larger batches of jerky, see the recipes in the next chapter.

Smoky Joe

Here's a jerky with a smoke flavor—without the smoke. It is especially good with top-quality lean beef, such as top round steak, thinly sliced. Cut it against the grain for normal use, or with the grain if you want a chew.

> 2 pounds lean red-meat steaks
> Liquid Smoke
> salt and black pepper

Partly freeze the steaks; this makes them easier to cut. Trim off all the fat, then slice the meat into strips about ¼ inch thick. Place the meat into a nonmetallic container, making a layer ½ inch thick. Sprinkle with salt, pepper, and Liquid Smoke. Add another layer of meat, another sprinkling, and so on, ending with the seasonings. Weight the meat with a plate or some such object. Cover and place into the refrigerator for 8 hours or so. Arrange the strips on a rack in a shallow baking pan or dish. Put into the oven at 140°F for 6 to 8 hours, or until dry. Cool the jerky and store it in airtight containers, preferably in the refrigerator or a cool place.

5

Teriyaki Jerky

This jerky can be made with a commercial teriyaki sauce, or you can mix your own with this recipe.

    2 pounds lean red meat
    ½ cup soy sauce
    ¼ cup brown sugar
    2 cloves garlic, crushed
    1 tablespoon salt
    1 tablespoon ground fresh gingerroot
    ½ teaspoon freshly ground black pepper

Cut the meat into strips ¼ inch thick. In a nonmetallic container, mix the rest of the ingredients and stir well. Add the meat a few strips at a time, tossing about to coat all sides with the teriyaki sauce. Cover and marinate in the refrigerator for 8 to 10 hours. Drain and dry in a kitchen oven at 140°F for 6 to 8 hours, or until dry.

A small batch of this jerky will probably be eaten right away—and in my house it is half gone before the drying process is complete. So, storage isn't a problem. For large batches that will be stored for a long time, vacuum-packed jars work best for me.

Barbecue Sauce Jerky

This jerky can be made with the aid of your favorite barbecue sauce, or you can use the recipe below.

    4 pounds lean red meat
    1 cup catsup
    ½ cup red wine vinegar

¼ cup brown sugar
2 tablespoons Worcestershire sauce
2 tablespoons salt
1 tablespoon dry mustard
½ tablespoon onion powder
1 teaspoon freshly ground black pepper
⅛ teaspoon Tabasco sauce

Trim the fat and tissue off the meat, then cut it into strips ½ inch thick. Mix all the other ingredients in a nonmetallic container. Add the meat, toss it about to coat all sides, and refrigerate for 10 hours or so. Drain the meat and place the strips on racks in a kitchen oven. Dry at 145°F for about 8 to 10 hours, or until the jerky is hardened to your liking. Store in sealed jars, preferably in the refrigerator, or in vacuum-packed containers.

Note: Some people call this "barbecued jerky." It isn't. A barbecued meat is juicy and soft and tender; jerky is dry and hard and tough, or very chewy.

Honey Jerky

The combination of honey, soy sauce, and lemon juice is not entirely lost in jerky. Be sure to try it, using regular soy sauce (with lots of salt). Also remember that honey is a natural food preservative.

2 pounds lean red meat
½ cup dark soy sauce
½ cup honey
¼ cup fresh lemon juice
2 cloves garlic, minced
1 teaspoon finely ground black pepper

Trim the meat and reduce it to strips ¼ inch thick. Mix the rest of the ingredients in a nonmetallic container. Dip the meat strips into the marinade mixture and put them into a nonmetallic container. Pour in what's left of the marinade. Cover and marinate for several hours in the refrigerator. Place the slices on a rack over a drip pan and dry at 150°F for 8 hours, or until the jerky is as dry as you like it. Store like ordinary jerky—but this won't last long.

Diane's Choice

My niece passed this recipe on to the rest of the family, saying that her children really love it. Well, uncles love it, too, and so does my dog Nosher. I don't have exact measures to offer. Just sprinkle on each ingredient, using what you think you need. Don't skimp on the salt, however.

    2 red-meat flank steaks
    seasoned salt
    garlic salt
    black pepper
    sugar
    Ac'cent
    Liquid Smoke

Slice the meat bacon-thin on a slant while it is half frozen. Sprinkle both sides with seasoned salt, garlic salt, black pepper, sugar, and Ac'cent. Brush with Liquid Smoke. Marinate in a glass container for 24 hours. Drain the meat and drape the strips over the oven racks. Dry for 15 minutes at the lowest setting. Turn off the oven, leaving the door closed, for 1 hour. Repeat the procedure two more times. Enjoy.

Mortonized Jerky

The Morton Salt Division of Morton Thiokol, Inc., markets a line of meat-curing salts and seasonings. The Tender Quick mix used in this recipe is widely available, usually sold in the canning section of supermarkets or from mail-order sources. The mix contains mostly salt, with small amounts of sodium nitrate, sodium nitrite, and other ingredients. In addition to curing the meat (mostly with the salt), the mix helps retain the color of red meat such as beef or venison. For more on curing salts, see "Jerky Ingredients and Safety" beginning on page 127.

2 pounds lean red meat
1 tablespoon Morton Tender Quick
2 teaspoons sugar
1 teaspoon black pepper
1 teaspoon garlic powder

Trim the meat and slice it with the grain into strips about 1½ inches wide and ½ inch thick. (Partly freezing the meat will make the slicing easier.) In a bowl, mix the other ingredients. Rub the slices of meat on all sides with the cure and spice mix, using all of it. Place the strips in a plastic bag and seal. Refrigerate for 1 hour. Then rinse the strips in cold water and pat dry with paper towels. Place the strips on greased racks in shallow baking pans. Do not allow the meat to overlap or touch. Place the pans in the oven and set the temperature as low as you can get it—120°F to 150°F. Dry for 8 hours or longer with the oven door cracked open. Cool and place the jerky into airtight jars or bags. Store in a cool place or freeze until needed.

Low-Salt Pepper Jerky

Here's a tasty jerky for people who feel a need to avoid salty fare. Be sure to use low-salt soy sauce, because most regular soy sauce is very high in salt. The measures below are for a modest amount of jerky, intended to be eaten right away. I don't recommend long storage under less-than-ideal conditions for low-salt jerky.

> 2 pounds lean red meat
> 1 cup low-salt soy sauce
> ¼ cup Liquid Smoke
> freshly ground black pepper

Cut the meat into strips ⅜ inch thick. Mix the Liquid Smoke and low-salt soy sauce in a large plastic bag. Add the meat, shaking it a little to coat all sides. Marinate for several hours in the refrigerator. Arrange the meat on racks for the oven. Sprinkle with freshly ground black pepper to taste; turn each strip and sprinkle the other side. Dry at 155°F for 6 hours or longer, depending on how hard you want the jerky.

Sesame Seed Jerky

Here's an Asian-style jerky made with sesame seeds. I especially like it while it is still warm from the oven.

> 2 pounds red-meat flank steak
> ½ cup soy sauce
> ½ cup sake, sherry, or dry vermouth
> ¼ cup sesame seeds
> 1 tablespoon brown sugar

1 tablespoon salt
½ teaspoon freshly ground black pepper (fine)

Mix all the ingredients except the meat and sesame seeds in a nonmetallic container; stir well. Cut the meat into strips about ¼ inch thick or a little thinner. Put the meat into the container, tossing it about to coat all sides. Cover the container and marinate overnight in the refrigerator, stirring a time or two. Drain the meat and arrange the strips on racks. Sprinkle the strips with the sesame seeds and dry for 6 hours or so at 140°F, or until dry to your liking.

Hawaiian Jerky

Pineapple juice helps this island recipe along. For a variation, use a can or two of chunk pineapple instead of juice. Pour off the juice for use in the jerky. Marinate and dry the chunks of pineapple right along with the meat.

2 pounds lean red meat
½ cup pineapple juice
½ cup soy sauce
2 cloves garlic, crushed
2 tablespoons brown sugar
1 tablespoon grated fresh gingerroot
1 tablespoon salt
1 teaspoon black pepper
½ teaspoon cayenne pepper

Mix all the ingredients except the meat in a nonmetallic container. Slice the meat into strips about ¼ inch thick. Add the meat to the container, tossing to coat all sides. Marinate in the refrigerator

11

overnight. Dry the strips in the oven on a low setting for 8 to 10 hours, or until the jerky is ready to your liking.

Chinese Jerky

Jerky is enjoyed as noshing fare in China, where it is often made on the sweet side, as in this recipe. Try it for a change.

2 pound red-meat flank steak
1 cup sugar
½ cup soy sauce
¼ cup catsup
¼ cup hoisin sauce
¼ cup oyster sauce
¼ cup honey
¼ cup sake, sherry, or dry vermouth
2 tablespoons salt

Slice the meat thinly—about ⅛ inch thick. Mix the rest of the ingredients in a nonmetallic container. Add the beef strips, tossing about to coat all sides. Marinate for 24 hours or longer in the refrigerator. Rig for drying in an oven at 250°F. Place the beef strips on drying trays. Dry for 45 minutes to 1 hour. It's best to eat this jerky warm, or save it for a few days. The recipe is not designed for long storage.

Dried-Herb Jerky

If you like the flavors of mixed herbs, try this recipe. It works best with finely powdered dried herbs.

2 pounds lean red meat
1 tablespoon salt
1 teaspoon onion salt
½ teaspoon garlic salt
½ teaspoon lemon-pepper seasoning salt
½ teaspoon oregano
½ teaspoon basil
½ teaspoon marjoram
½ teaspoon thyme

Trim the meat and cut it into strips about ³⁄₁₆ inch thick. Thoroughly mix all the dry ingredients and sprinkle onto one side of each beef strip, using about half of the mixture. Pound the strips with a meat tenderizer, working in the spices. Turn the strips and sprinkle with the rest of the dry mix. Arrange the strips on racks and dry in the oven at about 140°F, with the door ajar, for 4 hours. Turn the strips and dry for another 4 to 6 hours, until the jerky bends the way you want it. Wrap each piece in paper towels and store in a jar.

Flank Steak Jerky

The flank of beef and other large animals makes an excellent jerky and can be prepared without actually cutting the meat with a knife—the way of some primitive peoples. According to Linda West Eckhardt's The Only Texas Cookbook *(the source of this recipe), some Mexican cooks use this method. The idea is to tear off strips of meat with the grain, and, of course, flank steak is ideal for this method. Note also that this method keeps the heat at about 200°F, which is higher than most practitioners recommend.*

flank steak
garlic
salt and black pepper

Put the flank steak into the freezer until it is partly frozen but still pliable. Tear off small strips with your hands. Pound each meat strip slightly with a wooden spoon or wooden spatula, flattening it. Rub each piece of meat with minced garlic (use about 1 clove of garlic to each pound of meat). Sprinkle the meat lightly on both sides with salt and pepper. Place the flattened strips on a rack in a baking pan. Place the pan in the center of the 200°F oven. Bake for 5 or 6 hours, turning once, or until each piece is dry to the touch but still pliable. Place the cooled jerky in jars, cover, and store in a dark place.

2

ELECTRIC DEHYDRATOR JERKY

Modern electric dehydrators, made primarily for drying slices of fruits and vegetables, have proved to be ideal for making jerky. They look small when compared to kitchen stove ovens, but the tightly spaced trays hold lots of jerky strips. The dehydrators are fitted with thermostats that control the temperatures to jerky-making and fruit-drying ranges, usually from 80°F to 150°F. In other words, they don't get too hot. Most dehydrators provide a constant flow of fan-forced air around the jerky, which helps promote even heating and exhaust the moisture from the unit.

The trays are a big part of the convenience, and anyone who sets out to build a wooden-box-type cold-smoker or dehydrator should look into the possibility of using store-bought trays designed for dehydrators. Most of the units are made of a tough plastic, although stainless-steel dehydrator trays are also available. In either case, the trays have a mesh bottom that allows the air to contact both sides of the meat.

All in all, the units are very easy to use—almost foolproof. Moreover, they operate at about 500 watts, a little more or less, which makes them inexpensive. It's about like burning five 100-watt lightbulbs.

There are two basic types of electric dehydrators, with two shapes of trays.

Round. These units feature round trays that stack atop each other. Usually these come with four or five trays, but additional trays can be purchased for some models. One unit of my acquaintance permits the use of up to fifteen trays—which will make lots of jerky. The total capacity, however, also depends on the diameter of the trays. These round dehydrators are widely available, and the cheaper models can be purchased in most discount stores. One potential problem with some of these units is that the air flow is from bottom to top, which means there may be a difference in temperature and humidity from one tray to another. Rotating the trays during drying helps.

Rectangular. Usually more expensive than the round dehydrators, these units feature a box with close-fitting, removable, drawerlike trays. The rectangular shape works a little better for loading strips of jerky, for the same reason that a square skillet works better than a round one for frying bacon. Several sizes are available, varying in the number and size of the trays. Usually the trays are plastic, but one large model has metal mesh trays. One disadvantage of the design is that more trays can't be added once the unit is full. On the other hand, trays can be removed to make enough head space to hold thick chunks of meat. In most of these units, the heat flows from the side, across the trays, rather than from the bottom up. This promotes even heating and drying, with no need to rotate the trays, which works a little better for unattended jerky making. The more expensive models come with a timer as well as a thermostat.

• • •

All of the recipes in the previous chapter can be made in a dehydrator instead of a kitchen oven. Easier, really, partly because the trays are so perfect for jerky. The recipes in the first chapter are designed for making small batches. The ones below, however, are for making larger amounts of jerky, partly because the larger dehydrators process more meat at a time. As a rule, any of the jerky recipes in this book can be scaled up or down, depending on the meat at hand and the equipment available. In some cases—usually when jerking large batches of meat—it may be desirable to choose recipes that work both with and without marinades or rubs. In other words, start using the dehydrator immediately to make a batch of jerky while part of the meat is being marinated.

Easy Big-Batch Jerky

Here's a big-batch recipe that's really hard to beat. Note that most of the salt used in the recipe comes from soy sauce. Do not use low-salt soy.

> 10 pounds lean meat, cut into strips ¼ inch thick
> 2 cups soy sauce
> 1 cup Worcestershire sauce
> ¼ cup Liquid Smoke
> salt and black pepper to taste

Mix all the liquid ingredients in a nonmetallic container. Add the meat, tossing about to coat all sides, cover, and refrigerate overnight. Drain the meat and arrange it on dehydrator trays. Salt and pepper the strips lightly and dry at 140°F for half an hour or so. Turn, sprinkle lightly with salt and pepper, and dry for 6 to 8 hours, or until dry to your taste and needs.

Smoky Jerky

Here's a good basic recipe for people who want a smoky flavor from dehydrator jerky.

10 pounds lean red meat, thinly sliced
2 cups Liquid Smoke
2 cups Worcestershire sauce
2 cups soy sauce
¼ cup salt
2 tablespoons garlic powder
1 tablespoon black pepper

Mix all the ingredients except the meat in a nonmetallic container. Add the meat, tossing about to coat all sides. Marinate in the refrigerator overnight. Drain the jerky, blot dry with paper towels, and arrange the strips on dehydrator trays. Dry at 140°F for 6 to 8 hours, or until done to your liking. Cool and store in glass Mason jars or airtight plastic bags, preferably using a vacuum-pack system.

Curing-Salt Jerky

Commercial curing mixes usually contain small amounts of sodium nitrate and sodium nitrite, both of which will impart a reddish color to the meat. The color isn't as important in jerky as it is in corned beef or cured ham, but some people want it. For more information, see the section in appendix A, "Jerky Ingredients and Safety."

10 pounds lean red meat
⅔ cup Morton Tender Quick cure
¼ cup sugar
2 tablespoons black pepper
1 tablespoon garlic powder

Cut the meat into slices ¼ inch thick. Thoroughly mix the dry ingredients. Rub the mix into the meat slices, covering all surfaces.

Place the meat into a nonmetallic container and refrigerate for 1 hour. Rinse the meat under running water and let it dry. Place the strips over dehydrator racks. Dry at 145°F for 8 hours or longer, depending on how hard you want the jerky.

Sweet Pickle Jerky

A good many brine cures call for sugar or brown sugar. Often sugar-cured jerky is smoked, but it can also be made in a dehydrator.

> 10 pounds lean red meat
> 2 gallons hot water
> 2 cups salt
> 1 cup brown sugar
> ¼ cup black pepper
> 1 tablespoon freshly ground allspice berries

Cut the meat into strips about ¼ inch thick. Mix the other ingredients in a nonmetallic container and cool. Add the meat, swishing it around to coat all sides. Keep in a cool place overnight. Rinse the strips in running water and drain. Place the strips over racks and dry at 140°F for 10 hours or until dry to your liking. Store in airtight containers, preferably vacuum-packed, until needed.

Chili Powder Jerky

This recipe for 10 pounds of meat can be doubled as needed, or it can be reduced. The chili powder can be purchased in the spice section of the supermarket. An 8-ounce can or two 4-ounce cans will be about 1 cup. This jerky makes a nice chew, and don't forget to try it cooked in a stew with pinto beans if you like chili with beans. (See chapter 12 for recipes for cooking with jerky.)

10 pounds lean red meat
1 cup prepared chili powder
½ cup salt
1 tablespoon freshly ground black pepper
1 tablespoon freshly ground cumin seeds
1 tablespoon garlic powder
½ tablespoon cayenne pepper

Mix all the dry ingredients. Trim the meat and cut it into strips about ⅜ inch thick and 1 inch wide, cutting with the grain if you want a chewy jerky, or across the grain for pemmican. Blot the moisture from the meat with paper towels. Rub the spice mix into the meat on all sides. Place in a nonmetallic container, cover, and refrigerate all night. Pat with paper towels to remove any surface moisture. Process the meat in a dehydrator (or kitchen oven) at 145°F for 4 hours. Lower the heat to 120°F and dry for another 4 hours or longer, until the meat is hard but not brittle. Vacuum-pack for long storage.

Wooster Jerky, Hot

Here's an easy recipe, making use of Worcestershire sauce and soy sauce. These staples can be purchased from Sam's Club and other warehouse outfits in gallon bottles at considerable savings.

10 pounds lean red meat, cut into strips ¼ inch thick
3 cups soy sauce
2 cups Worcestershire sauce
½ cup Liquid Smoke
¼ cup freshly ground black pepper

Put the meat into a nonmetallic container. Add the rest of the ingredients, mixing thoroughly. Refrigerate for several hours, or overnight, tossing or turning a time or two. Dry at 140°F for about 8 hours, or until done to your liking.

Note: Do not use low-salt soy sauce for this recipe. If you do, add some salt.

No-Fuss Jerky with Barbecue Sauce

This is a jerky that requires no complicated soaks or rubs. You don't even have to measure the ingredients, if you have a little experience with cooking or jerky making. It's best to use a tomato-based barbecue sauce, available in any supermarket these days. Some markets carry it in gallon jugs, which usually make it quite economical. Please, however, don't call the results of this recipe "barbecued jerky." All true barbecue is moist and succulent; all true jerky, dry and chewy. For best results, cut the meat into strips about 1/16 inch thick, but thicker jerky will work.

    thinly sliced red-meat strips
    barbecue sauce
    garlic salt
    onion salt

Arrange the strips of meat on the drying trays without overlapping. Brush each strip lightly with the sauce and sprinkle with garlic and onion salts. Dry at 140°F for 3 or 4 hours. Turn the strips and brush lightly with more sauce. Dry for another 3 or 4 hours, or until dry to your liking. This jerky will keep for several days, preferably in the refrigerator.

Big-Batch Hawaiian Jerky

Here's a nice mild jerky for sweet chewing.

10 pounds lean red meat
2½ cups pineapple juice
2½ cups soy sauce
¼ cup brown sugar
¼ cup grated fresh gingerroot
10 cloves garlic, crushed
3 tablespoons salt
3 tablespoons ground ginger (dry)
1 tablespoon black pepper
½ tablespoon cayenne pepper

Cut the meat into strips ¼ inch thick, or a little thinner. Mix all the ingredients except the meat, stirring well. Put the meat into a nonmetallic container. Pour the marinade over the meat, tossing the mixture about with your hands to coat all sides. Cover and marinate overnight in the refrigerator, stirring a time or two if convenient. Drain the strips and arrange them in dehydrator trays. Dry at 140°F for 6 to 8 hours, or until done to your liking. Store in an airtight container in the refrigerator for a few days. Freeze for longer storage.

Note: Kids love this jerky recipe—and I do, too.

3

CAMP AND OLD-TIME JERKY

You don't have to use a kitchen oven or an electric dehydrator to make jerky. In fact, the best jerky might well be made out in the sun or in a dry, breezy open-air place. Open-air jerky, made without the aid of a little heat of some sort, works best when the humidity is quite low. So, choose a dry climate or watch your local weather report for the proper conditions, which will usually be during periods of high pressure.

I might add that most writers on the subject do not recommend the old ways of making jerky under any circumstances. I won't go that far, but there are some precautions. First, do not hang jerky out in the open if flies are a problem. Second, do not attempt to air-dry jerky when the humidity is high. Third, proceed only with very, very fresh and uncontaminated meat. Fourth, use lots of salt. Fifth, hang the jerky in a breezy place, if possible. Sixth, do not allow the jerky to get wet during the drying process.

In addition to open-air drying, the complete outdoor cook may want to use large covered grills or various "smokers" to make jerky. Essentially, these are more or less closed systems, not unlike ovens or dehydrators in principle. Often a little smoke is used to flavor the jerky. In general, the big problem is keeping the temperature hot enough to generate smoke but low enough to prevent the jerky from cooking. Another problem is getting the water vapor from the meat out of the smoker or closed grill. Further instruction is provided in the recipes below.

Indian Jerky

If you want a long strip of jerky, making it easier to hang, you might try an old American Indian trick. Place a partly frozen round steak of buffalo or beef about ¾ inch thick on a flat surface. Start your cut around the edge of the meat. Cut carefully, working in a spiral, until you get to the center. This will give you a continuous strip of meat—easily hung from a clothesline. Dry in the sun for several days, depending on the heat and humidity. Take it into the tepee at night or during the rain, hanging it high above the fire.

8th Virginia Jerky

I found this recipe in a booklet called Confederate Camp Cooking, *by Patricia B. Mitchell. It calls for smoking the jerky for 6 hours in a covered grill, which I doubt was standard camp equipment. It also calls for a "dash" of Liquid Smoke, but I'm not sure that this stuff would have been readily available to a Confederate soldier. In any case, I don't see the point in using both Liquid Smoke and real smoke. My guess is that a Confederate soldier would simply suspend the meat well above the campfire, using the heat to dry the meat and counting on the smoke to keep the insects away. On the other hand, maybe the seasoned Reb wouldn't want to risk much of a fire, lest the smoke draw Yankees.*

    1 pound lean red meat
    1 tablespoon salt
    1 teaspoon red pepper
    1 teaspoon black pepper
    1 teaspoon garlic powder
    ⅛ teaspoon Liquid Smoke
    1 cup water

Trim the meat of fat and cut it into thin strips, then put these into a nonmetallic container. Mix the rest of the ingredients and pour over the meat. Toss about to coat all sides. Marinate in a cool place overnight. Smoke for 6 hours or longer "in a covered grill." Modern practitioners can use a large covered grill, putting the fire and wood chips in one end and the meat in the other. Choke off the airflow, thereby reducing the heat.

Vietnamese Grilled Sun-Dried Jerky

Fresh lemongrass is becoming more readily available in American super-markets as well as in Asian stores, and it can be grown in the home herb garden in mild climates. The outer leaves of the stalk should be peeled away, down to the inner core, about ½ inch in diameter. This core is then thinly sliced and will impart a lemony flavor to food. The red meat (usually beef) for this recipe should be sliced very thin in the pieces about 3 inches wide and 3 inches long, more or less.

> 1 pound lean red meat
> 2 stalks fresh lemongrass, thinly sliced
> 3 tablespoons light soy sauce
> 2 tablespoons brown sugar
> 1 tablespoon Vietnamese fish sauce
> 2 small red chili peppers, seeded and minced

Using a mortar and pestle, pound together the red chili peppers and sugar. Add the lemongrass, soy sauce, and fish sauce, mixing well. Spread the paste over both sides of the meat slices. Marinate for 30 minutes. Spread the slices on drying racks and place in the sun for about 10 hours, until both sides are dry. Cover at night or during a rain. (I put my jerky on dehydrator trays and dry in the sun, or start in the sun and finish in the dehydrator on a low temperature, if necessary.) When dry, grill the strips of meat over charcoal for a few minutes, until nicely crisp. Serve as a snack with sticky rice. The grilled jerky can be stored for a week or two in the refrigerator.

South African *Biltong*

This is the jerky of South Africa, made commercially as well as in the home, especially in rural areas. Biltong is eaten as a snack, sold at refreshment stands in movie theaters and at soccer games and wayside stands; it is also sometimes used as a flavoring or ingredient in recipes for home cooking. Coriander seeds, freshly ground, give it a special flavor. Note that the meat is cured in a cool dry place, not in a warm oven. The ingredients list calls for beef or venison, but other meats can also be used. According to the Best of Regional African Cooking, *"You can buy biltong of beef or springbok (a South African antelope) or even ostrich. The latter, South Africans will tell you, is the best."*

> 10 pounds lean red meat
> 1 pound coarse salt
> 3 tablespoons freshly ground coriander seeds
> 2 tablespoons freshly ground black pepper
> 1 ounce saltpeter (see appendix A)
> brine (see appendix A)

Cut the meat with the grain into strips about ⅜ inch thick. Thoroughly mix the coarse salt, saltpeter, coriander, and black pepper, making sure that the saltpeter is evenly distributed. Rub most of the spice mixture into the strips of meat. Layer the strips in a crock or nonmetallic container and sprinkle the top with the rest of the spice mix. Refrigerate or keep in a cool place for 48 hours or longer. Mix a strong brine, using enough salt to float an egg. Rinse the meat in the brine and hang it in a cool, well-ventilated place until it dries thoroughly. This makes a superb chew.

See also the next recipe, which produces a thicker jerky.

East African *Biltong*

Although South Africa is the biltong capital, the stuff is also widely eaten in most of eastern Africa, where it is sold by street vendors along with fruits and other snacks and delicacies, such as roasted termites.

    10 pounds lean red meat
    1 pound salt
    2 ounces sugar
    1 ounce saltpeter
    dried red chili peppers, ground finely

Trim the fat off the meat and cut it into strips about 1 inch thick. Mix the rest of the ingredients thoroughly. Rub the mixture into the meat, covering all sides, and put it into a nonmetallic container. Sprinkle any leftover rub over the meat. Marinate for 2 days in a cool place, tossing the strips a time or two. Dip a clean cloth in vinegar, wring out the excess, and wipe the meat strips. Hang the strips in a cool, airy, dry place for several days, until the jerky is dry. In case rainy weather develops, this jerky can be finished in a kitchen oven on very low heat, or in a dehydrator.

Survival Jerky According to Herter

Knowing how to make this jerky might save the day in case of an atomic bomb attack, says George Leonard Herter in the book

27

Bull Cook and Authentic Historical Recipes and Practices, at which time our electric freezers and meat dehydrators wouldn't help. Rig for smoke-drying by building a log tower, Herter says, about 3 feet square and open at the top. Place 1-inch-diameter green branches over the top, forming a rack. Cut the meat into strips ½ inch thick, 1 inch wide, and 10 or 12 inches long. Place these strips on the rack. Keep a slow, smoldering fire going in the bottom, preferably using hickory, mesquite, or maple wood. Smoke for about 12 hours, or until the meat is dry. If a log tower isn't practical, use a hole in the ground with a rack on top, Herter says.

Before eating, soak the jerky in water for 4 or 5 hours, or, better, simmer the jerky in a stew along with vegetables. If no vegetables are available, Herter advises, use wild grape leaves, aspen leaves, laurel leaves, or the bark from small pine trees. I might add that the inner bark of a pine tree is by far better than the outer scale. Further recipes for using the jerky are set forth in chapters 11 and 12.

Alaskan Cabin Jerky

Woodstoves are still being used for heat and cooking, especially in remote areas. The heat of the stove causes the air to rise, creating a sort of open dehydrator for making jerky and drying the long johns.

2 pounds lean red meat
¾ cup water
3 tablespoons salt
½ tablespoon onion powder
¼ tablespoon garlic powder
¼ tablespoon black pepper
1 teaspoon cayenne pepper

Trim the meat and cut it into slices about ³⁄₁₆ inch thick. Mix the rest of the ingredients in a jar, shaking well. Put the meat into a nonmetallic container and pour the contents of the jar over it, tossing about to coat all sides. Let sit in a cool place for several hours. Dry the meat strips with paper towels and place them on racks in the oven on low heat for half an hour or so. The purpose of the stay in the oven is to dry the meat a little to reduce the drip. Do not cook the meat in a hot oven. Hang the meat strips on the clothesline above the stove for a day or two. If there's any jerky left hanging after 2 days, store it in a jar or a clean pillowcase.

West Texas Porch Jerky

Many ranch houses have screened porches on the front or back, or both. Some even have porches all the way around. In dry climates with a good wind, these screened porches can be used to make excellent jerky. String some barbed wire across the top and hang the strips of meat from the barbs. In some parts of the West, small wild peppers are free for the picking. Any dried hot red chili peppers can be used, ground to a powder. Cayenne from the supermarket will do; or use a commercial chili powder, if you like the taste of cumin and other spices.

> 5 pounds lean red meat
> salt
> wild chili peppers, dried and powdered

Trim the meat and cut it into strips about ¼ inch thick. Sprinkle the meat strips liberally with salt and sparsely with powdered chili peppers, put them into a nonmetallic container, and keep in a cool place overnight, tossing a time or two if convenient. Drain the meat, pat the strips dry, and impale each strip by the end on the barbs of the wire. Let it hang for 2 or 3 days, or longer, depending on the heat, wind, and humidity. Good stuff, weather permitting.

Clothesline Jerky

If you have a suitable climate—dry, warm, and breezy—you can make jerky by simply hanging it on the clothesline. It's best to punch a hole in the end of each jerky strip, insert a short length of cotton twine, and tie each strip to the main line with a loop. To separate one strip from another, the loop can be kept in place with a clothespin. If you don't have any string at hand, use strips of fiber from the blades of beargrass or other suitable yucca. You can also string up the jerky strips onto strong line, such as the fine-diameter Kevlar thread used in fly tying, with the aid of a large needle. Still another possibility is to string up sticker vines (such as catbrier) in a suitable place, open to sun and a light wind, and merely hang the strips on the spurs. Don't be tempted to hang the jerky strips on fishhooks, as when setting a trotline. If you do, you might catch a neighborhood dog.

    long meat strips, ³⁄₁₆ inch thick and 1 inch wide
    hickory-smoked salt (or regular salt)
    black pepper

Sprinkle both sides of the meat heavily with hickory salt and black pepper. Hang on the line as described above for 2 days or longer, depending on the climate and how dry you want the jerky. Lots of pepper will discourage flies and insects. Transfer the strips to a dry place during rain and at night.

Brine-Cured Smoked Jerky with Rub

Here's a good recipe for making smoked jerky, using both a brine and a rub.

The Meat and the Brine

5 pounds lean red meat
2 quarts spring water
1 cup salt
½ cup unsulfured molasses
¼ cup freshly ground black pepper
1 teaspoon bottled garlic juice

The Rub

½ cup fine sea salt
1 tablespoon dried lemon zest, powdered
½ tablespoon cayenne pepper

Trim and cut the meat into strips about ⅜ inch thick. Mix the rest of the brine ingredients in a nonmetallic container. Add the meat strips, tossing about to coat all sides. Cover and refrigerate for 8 hours or longer. Rinse the meat and pat it dry with absorbent paper. Air-dry the meat for about an hour.

While waiting, mix all the rub ingredients and then rub into both sides of the jerky strips. Arrange the strips in a smoker. Smoke the meat for an hour or so at 140°F or less. Continue drying without smoke until the strips are stiff but bendable. Cool and store until needed.

Water Smoker Jerky

Several kinds of water smokers, some shaped like a small silo, can be used to make jerky. These are usually rigged with a wood chip pan above a heat source (gas, charcoal, or electric) and a pan for holding water or other liquid. Most of these have two circular trays spaced far apart, which limits the amount of jerky that can be handled at one time. The temperature inside the smoker can also be a problem. The best jerky will be produced with the temperature at 140°F or lower. Also remember to keep any top vents open to promote air flow across the jerky.

> 2 pounds lean red meat
> salt
> black pepper
> hardwood chips

Cut the meat into strips about ¼ inch thick. Sprinkle the strips heavily on both sides with salt. Put into a nonmetallic container overnight, tossing a time or two. Rinse the strips in running water to remove some of the salt. Rig for smoking, heating some hardwood chips. Dry the meat strips with paper towels, sprinkle lightly with black pepper, and arrange on the racks. Smoke for several hours, then finish without smoke until the jerky is dry to your liking.

Electric Smoker Jerky

The several portable electric smokers will make good jerky if they are well ventilated to encourage a fresh air flow from the bottom to the top, along with the smoke. Temperature can be a problem. Check it with an oven thermometer, shooting for about 140°F or less. Most of these units have two pullout racks for holding large chunks of meat, which limits their capacity.

Check for availability of additional racks, or perhaps hang the jerky from the top by using toothpicks or some other method.

    2 pounds lean red meat
    bacon drippings (optional)
    hardwood chunks
    salt
    freshly ground black pepper or cayenne pepper

Rig for smoking, putting the hardwood chunks into the pan. Cut the meat into strips about ³⁄₁₆ inch thick. Brush the strips lightly with bacon drippings, then sprinkle with salt and lightly with black pepper or very lightly with cayenne. Place the strips over the racks, or hang them from the top rack. Smoke for several hours, then finish drying without adding more wood to the tray.

Note: Don't go too heavy on the bacon drippings, especially if the strips are to be hung. The purpose of the drippings is to help the beef take on a smoke flavor. They can be omitted, however.

Cold-Smoked Cured Jerky

Very good jerky can be made in a cold-smoker at 100°F or even lower. The problem here is getting enough heat for a fire to generate smoke while at the same time keeping the smoke chamber cool. Often the smoke chamber is removed from the fire, as in the familiar barrel placed uphill from a small fire and connected by a conduit of some sort. Several designs, as well as advice on woods and techniques for smoking, have been set forth in my book Cold-Smoking & Salt-Curing Meat, Fish, & Game, *if I may be blatant enough to refer to my own work. In any case, for cold-smoking I insist that the meat be salt-cured in one way or another. The recipe below has been adapted from an old Scottish recipe for corned beef. You can, in fact, use the chunks of meat for corned beef (simmered in fresh water for 5 or 6 hours, or until tender), or you can cut the meat, after curing, into strips, rinse them in fresh water, and cold-smoke them for a couple of days, until dry to your liking. You can also cut the meat into strips before curing, in which case the curing time would be shortened to 8 hours or so, or overnight.*

Many of the old-time recipes call for saltpeter, which is no longer used in commercially cured meats such as sausage. It is, however, still available over the counter in some pharmacies. See "Jerky Ingredients and Safety," appendix A, for notes on saltpeter and other cures.

lean red-meat roast, about 5 pounds
1 gallon spring water
1 pound salt
⅓ pound brown sugar
½ ounce saltpeter

Put all the ingredients except the meat into a large pot. Bring to a boil and simmer for 5 minutes. Strain the brine into a crock or other suitable nonmetallic container. Let cool. Trim the roast nicely and add it to the crock. Weight the roast with a clean block of wood or plate to keep it submerged. Cover the crock and put it in a cool place for 2 weeks. Turn the meat every day or two.

After 2 weeks, rinse the roast in cold water and soak it in fresh water for several hours. (To cook it like corned beef, put the meat into a pot, cover with cold water, and bring to a boil. Reduce the heat and simmer for about 40 minutes per pound, or until tender. The emphasis is on a simmer, not a hard boil. Serve the corned meat hot or cold, or use it in recipes that call for corned beef. When slicing the roast, it's best to cut against the grain.)

For jerky, rinse the roast in cold water, cut it into strips about ³⁄₁₆ inch thick, rinse the strips in fresh water, pat dry, and arrange on the trays of a cold-smoker, or hang if necessary. Cold-smoke until the strips are dry to your liking. The exact time will, of course, depend on the temperature, the humidity, and the thickness of the meat. Note also that the smoke doesn't have to be continuous during the drying process, unless perhaps insects would be a problem without the smoke.

Variations: Many recipes call for adding a long list of spices to the brine. I prefer to leave them out, but anyone who feels the need to alter the flavor might want to add 2 tablespoons mixed pickling spices, available in the spice or canning sections of supermarkets, and perhaps 1 tablespoon black pepper. About 2 heaping tablespoons allspice berries and a few bay leaves also work.

Big-Batch Cold-Smoking for Big Game

If you like the flavor of the jerky or corned beef made by the recipe above, remember that the process is quite suitable for larger quantities of meat and won't require quite as much brine per pound. Corning and smoking are good ways to deal with the sheer bulk of a steer, moose, or elk when your freezer is already full. The biggest problem with corning a big batch of meat will be finding a large crock and having a cool place to keep it. A clean wooden barrel can be used, if you have one.

> 100 pounds lean meat
> 5 gallons clean water
> 2 pounds brown sugar or honey
> 8 pounds salt
> 2 ounces saltpeter

Bone the meat and cut it into rather large chunks. Boil the water. Add all the ingredients except the meat and bring to a new boil.

35

Turn off the heat and let the water cool to 40°F or lower. Pack the meat loosely in the crock. Pour the brine into the crock and top the meat with a clean wooden block or platter, weighted with a clean stone (preferably flint) if necessary. The idea is to keep all the meat submerged. After several days, repack the meat, reversing the order; repeat this step every few days. Cure for about 2 weeks for 5-pound chunks of meat. Smaller pieces will require less time and should be eaten first. As a general rule, judge each piece of meat separately, allowing at least 3 days for each pound.

The fully corned meat will keep for a couple of months in the brine, depending partly on the storage temperature, but the brine should perhaps be drained off after about 20 days and replaced with a freshly made solution. For jerky, the meat can be cut into strips and cold-smoked or air-dried after the cure is complete, using the technique above for the small batch. Start jerking the smaller pieces of meat first, leaving the large chunks in the brine longer.

4

JERKY EVERY WHICH WAY

Jerky doesn't have to be made in thin strips like bacon. As a practical matter, slabs and chunks are often easier to cut than thin strips. Time spent in cutting the meat can be a factor, especially if you are working on a large volume, such as an elk or a beef hindquarter, without the help of an electric meat slicer or other professional tools. As a rule, however, large chunks of meat will take lots of time to dry.

Smaller chunks, like stew meat, can also be made into jerky and are much easier to chew. These can be made from round steak or other supermarket cuts, or they can be made from the trimmings left from cutting larger cuts of meat into thin jerky strips.

In any case, be sure to try these recipes and methods. The directions are for using a dehydrator, but a kitchen oven will also work.

A. D.'s Jerky Nuggets

Small chunks of jerky are perfect for eating while you are driving a car or on the trail, and for people who have trouble biting off a chew from a strip of tough jerky. The trick here is to simply plop a nugget into your mouth and roll it around with your tongue until it is soft enough to chew. I like to make this jerky from a large chunk of meat, such as a bottom round beef roast, but it can also be made quite easily by using a steak about 1 inch thick. Round steak will do, if nicely trimmed of fat and sinew.

5 pounds lean red meat
1 cup salt
½ cup brown sugar
1 tablespoon freshly ground black pepper

Dice the meat into 1-inch cubes, putting them into a nonmetallic tray or other suitable container. Mix the dry ingredients and sprinkle evenly over the meat. Toss the meat about to coat all sides. Cover and refrigerate for 48 hours, turning the meat a time or two each day. Rinse the meat, pat it dry, and arrange it on dehydrator trays. Dry at 120°F for 24 hours or longer, or until the meat is dry on the outside but still pliable inside. Store in an airtight container, preferably in the refrigerator.

Stew-Meat Jerky

These are similar to jerky nuggets, but the pieces can be more irregular. I make them from trimmings left from large chunks of meat, but very fresh supermarket stew meat (beef) can also be used. The pieces, however, should be rather uniform in thickness and should not be too large. If you use several sizes, it's best to sort them and put them on separate trays. The larger chunks will require more drying. If you purchase supermarket stew meat, make sure it is quite fresh, and be prepared to trim off any fat and sinew.

I don't normally use spices and seasonings in this jerky, partly because these can be added when making the stew. Of course, this jerky can also be used as a snack, in which case spices and flavorings may be added to taste.

stew-cut lean red meat
salt
black pepper

Put the meat in layers into a nonmetallic container, sprinkling each layer liberally with salt and sparsely with black pepper. Cover and put into the refrigerator for 24 hours. Rinse in clean water, pat dry with paper towels, and arrange on dehydrator racks. Dry at 120°F for a day or longer, until the meat is dry to your liking. For long storage without refrigeration, the jerky should be also dry inside.

See chapter 12 for suitable recipes for cooking with this jerky.

Jerky Plugs

At one time, country boys liked to keep a plug of tobacco in the bib pocket of their overalls. To take a chew, they simply sliced off a piece of tobacco from the end of the plug with the small blade of their pocketknife. The same technique can be used for jerky, and, boy, is it tasty. For meat, any good slab of low-fat red meat of suitable size will do. I sometimes use "breakfast steaks" as sold at my local supermarket. These are simply small steaks cut from eye of round. Larger plugs can be cut from other parts of the hind leg of beef. I like the thickness to be about 1 inch. Thinner slices will dry into plugs that are too thin. If properly prepared, these make a truly great jerky that seems to have more flavor than do strips. At least, they come to flavor more quickly, owing to the freshly cut surfaces.

> small steaks or cutlets lean red meat
> soy sauce
> Liquid Smoke
> salt
> black pepper

Place the meat onto a nonmetallic tray or other suitable container. Sprinkle both sides with soy sauce, Liquid Smoke, salt, and black pepper to taste. Cover and keep in a cool place for about 8 hours, or perhaps overnight, turning the steaks from time to time. Pat the steaks dry and place on dehydrator trays for 12 hours at 140°F, or until done to your liking. Wrap each piece separately with paper towels and store in an airtight container until needed.

Note: These plugs can also be used for cooking some of the recipes in chapter 12.

Foxfire Jerky

Several people contributed to the section on dried beef in the book Foxfire 11. *This account relies heavily on the method reported by Garnet Lovell, who used rather large chunks of meat from the hindquarter. "And you'd never cut it into strips," he said, because they don't "have the flavor."*

> beef or other lean red meat in chunks of about 5 pounds each
> plenty of salt

Sprinkle the chunks of meat on all sides with plenty of salt. Put the meat in a dry place for about 2 days, or until it stops sweating. (If the weather is humid, the process will take a week or so, in which case the practicality of using the method should be questioned.) After the meat has "taken the salt," as they say in *Foxfire* country, cut a hole in the small end and slide in a sweet birch stick to hang it by. Hang it about 6 feet above a fireplace for about 4 weeks, or longer for larger pieces. When the meat dries, put it in cloth bags (clean flour sacks or pillowcases will do) and hang it in a dry place.

Another *Foxfire* contributor said to wrap the meat in cheesecloth, then hang it over the woodstove in the kitchen to dry.

How was the meat eaten in *Foxfire* country? According to Blanche Lovell, you slice off pieces the thickness of a 50-cent piece.

Soak the pieces in water until they are soft. Dust in flour and dry in a skillet—cast iron, of course.

Charqui Mendoza

For the information used in this text (adapted from my book *Cold-Smoking & Salt-Curing Meat, Fish, & Game*), I stand head over heels in debt to *The South American Cook Book,* written half a century ago by Cora, Rose, and Bob Brown. Cured beef and other red-meat jerky are popular in many areas south of the Rio Grande, and it is an important part of the national cuisine of both Argentina and Brazil.

I might add that salt-dried red meat is called *charqui* in several South American countries. Some people have argued that our word *jerky* comes from *charqui,* possibly going back to a pre-Inca Indian tribe in the Andes and foothills. In Brazil, the word is *xarque;* in the Spanish-speaking West Indies, *tasajo.*

Of course, there are a number of variations on making *charqui.* Here is a technique used in Mendoza, Argentina, where, according to the Browns, not only beef but also guanaco and rhea are made into *charqui.* (Of course, you can use North American venison or buffalo or even beef to make the jerky; also, our farmers and speculators are now raising the emu and ostrich as well as the rhea, so that these good red meats will be in our markets in the future if all goes according to plan. Meanwhile, you might be able to snare a wild rhea with a bola the next time you go trout fishing in Argentina.)

Anyhow, to make the *charqui,* first select tender parts of meat and butcher it into large pieces. Slice the pieces into thin steaks and put them under a press to squeeze out the excess juice. Rub coarse salt into the meat on both sides. Natural sea salt is best, I think, because it has a good flavor and contains minerals that aid in the

41

curing process. After salting, stack the pieces on top of each other in a cool place and let stand for 24 hours. Dry the pieces with paper towels and expose them to the air, covered with a wire screen. After 5 days, put the steaks onto a flat surface and pound them with a wooden mallet. Repeat the pounding two or three times. Then store the *charqui* in fresh, cool, dry air. Remember that Mendoza is in the piedmont area of Argentina, not in the moist pampas around Buenos Aires. Climate makes a big difference.

In South America, jerky isn't merely a trail nibble to be taken along in the backpack. It's still a staple for the family, used almost every day in stews of one sort or another. It is usually soaked overnight in water to freshen it, then put into the stew pot the following day. In Chile, for example, *charquican* (a stew made from *charqui*) contains potatoes, green peas, string beans, yellow squash, chili pepper, onion, tomato, green corn, and *charqui*. So, make up a batch and try it in your favorite stew recipe—or in camp chili, made with only *charqui,* chili powder, tomato paste, and water. It's hard to beat a thick *charqui* chili served on a plate with black beans, white rice, and chopped onions, mixing it all together as you eat. See also chapter 12 for several applicable recipes.

5

GROUND-MEAT JERKY

Although jerky is traditionally made from solid strips, ground meat offers a way to use scraps and odd cuts. Moreover, burger jerky, if properly made, is of uniform size and shape. It is also quite tasty—and easier to chew than solid strips. There is a thin line here between jerky and small dried sausage such as Slim Jims. Of course, if the meat is stuffed into a natural (gut) or artificial casing, it becomes a sausage. As a rule, jerky is flat, not round.

The first step toward acceptable burger jerky is to obtain good low-fat ground meat. Forget off-the-shelf supermarket ground meat, which almost always contains quite a bit of fat and sometimes, if we may believe newspaper accounts, *E. coli* and other bacteria. It is almost always safer and better to grind your own meat. Start with a large chunk of meat that is relatively fat-free, such as roasts cut from the hind leg of beef.

After you obtain a large chunk of good red meat, rig your meat grinder. I use an ordinary hand-cranked sausage mill with a ³⁄₁₆- or ⅛-inch wheel. Electric meat grinders will do just fine. In either case, sterilize the grinder parts with boiling water. With clean rubber gloves on your hands, cut the meat with a sharp knife into chunks suitable for feeding the hopper of the grinder. Spread the meat chunks out on a clean surface and sprinkle them evenly with the seasonings. Then grind the chunks slowly, letting the meat fall into a sterilized container as it comes out. Note that the meat is not touched by hand during the grinding process.

Of course, smaller cuts of supermarket meat, such as round beef steaks or even stew meat, can be used—but with added risk. Market-ground meat can be relatively safe to eat, if you know and trust the butcher. But meat ground in one location in large batches, packaged, and shipped around the country should be avoided. The larger the batch, the more likely it is that the meat will be contaminated, for the same reason that it's better to keep your apples in several small baskets than to put them into a large barrel.

I prefer to proceed with meat fresh from the farm or, better, from the hunt, but many people consider this unsafe because the meat hasn't been "inspected" by the USDA. I might add, however, that government experts and meat processors will be quick to point out that wild meat may be tainted. Suit yourself. Just remember that most jerky is not really cooked.

Anyhow, after you obtain good ground meat, you'll have to form it into thin strips or perhaps nuggets. There are several ways of doing this:

Jerky Shooters. These handy gadgets are available commercially for extruding ground meat from a cylinder onto drying trays. Basically, they work like caulking guns. The meat is loaded into a cylinder. A plunger operated with a ratchet trigger forces the meat through a flattened tip, causing the meat to ooze out in a thin ribbon of uniform thickness and width. These strips can be squeezed out directly onto dehydrator trays. Some oven racks, however, may be spaced too widely for easy use, in which case a finer-mesh rack or even a solid sheet must be used. It's best to avoid, if possible, having to transfer the strips from one surface to another, because they come apart easily.

Most of the jerky guns have interchangeable tips, from wide and thin to small and round, Slim Jim style. Most of these tips can be used for jerky, but, of course, those thin strips are more conventional and are easier to dry.

In addition to handheld guns, several commercial extruders are available, some of which fit directly onto the grinding machine. At the other extreme, some home cooks may already have pastry bags with ribbon tips, and these may do the trick if the ground meat is of the right consistency.

In any case, the texture of the meat has a bearing on how nicely it extrudes. Sometimes grinding the meat with a smaller wheel, or grinding it a second time with a regular wheel, will make it easier to use—but don't make it mushy enough to lose its shape after being extruded. Much depends on the grind, the extruder, and the kind of meat.

Rolling Pins. Many people roll a mound of ground meat out into a sheet, like pizza dough. The thickness of the meat can be controlled almost exactly by putting one thin strip of wood on each side of the meat; the wood, of course, prevents the rolling pin from going too deep. (Try strips of ¼- or ⅜-inch plywood or paneling.) After being rolled out, the meat sheet is cut into strips with a knife or cutting wheel. Usually, the meat is rolled out on waxed paper, then transferred to a cookie sheet or some other surface for drying. The big problem is keeping the strips together, for they stick to the surface and tear easily.

In one method, put the meat between two sheets of waxed paper and roll until it is about ¼ inch thick. Both sheets are placed onto a cookie sheet. Carefully remove the top paper. Put the sheet into the oven on low heat—120°F—and leave it for about 2 hours. Place a second cookie sheet on top, flip the whole thing over, and remove the first cookie sheet and waxed paper. The drying continues for another hour or so. When the meat is firm and pliable, cut it into strips with kitchen shears. The strips are then dried—preferably on racks—at 140°F until done to your liking. Blot any grease off the jerky, cool, and store in a cool place in glass jars, preferably vacuum-packed.

Press Method. Several jerky presses are available commercially. Typically, these simply squeeze a ball or blob of ground meat down to a flat sheet, which in turn is cut into jerky strips. If you have a tortilla press, use it to make small wheels. You can also press the meat between sheets of waxed paper, using a flat surface and a flat pan or other suitable moveable object. The difficulty with the press method is that the jerky sheets tend to stick to the surfaces of the press.

Finger Method. If you want chunk jerky, simply shape the meat into small balls and place them onto dehydrator trays or fine-mesh oven trays. These can be flattened somewhat before being placed on the trays, if you want patties. Also try rolling a little jerky by hand into small logs.

Most good jerky recipes can be adapted in one way or another to ground meat. Marinades and long-standing rubs should be applied to the meat, perhaps in chunks, prior to grinding. Also try your favorite sausage recipes for jerky, perhaps making both from the same grind. Here are a few other recipes to try.

Shooter Jerky

The measures for this recipe can easily be adapted for larger batches of meat. For 10 pounds of meat, simply multiply everything by 5.

2 pounds ground lean red meat
6 tablespoons soy sauce
2 tablespoons Worcestershire sauce
½ teaspoon freshly ground black pepper
½ teaspoon powdered onion
¼ teaspoon powdered garlic
¼ teaspoon freshly ground nutmeg
¼ teaspoon powdered ginger

Cut the meat into cubes suitable for feeding into a sausage mill. Place the cubes into a nonmetallic container, pour in the soy sauce, and Worcestershire, toss about to cover all sides, cover, and marinate overnight in the refrigerator, turning a time or two. Spread the meat cubes out over a clean surface. Mix all the dry ingredients and sprinkle evenly over the meat cubes. Grind the meat, using a ³⁄₁₆- or ⅛-inch wheel. Stuff some of the meat into a jerky gun with a wide nozzle attached. Extrude the meat in strips directly onto dehydrator trays. Dry at 140°F for 6 to 8 hours or longer, depending partly on how long you plan to keep the jerky.

Note: This recipe also works with the rolling-pin method.

Ground-Meat Jerky

Use only very fresh or frozen, lean meat for this recipe. Partly thaw the meat before proceeding.

4 pounds lean red meat
1 cup soy sauce
¼ cup Worcestershire sauce
1 tablespoon Tabasco sauce
1 tablespoon freshly ground black pepper
1 tablespoon garlic powder
1 tablespoon Liquid Smoke (optional)

Trim the meat closely, cut it into chunks, and spread it out, tightly packed, on a clean surface. Sprinkle the black pepper and garlic powder over the meat. Mix all the liquid ingredients, then sprinkle them evenly over the meat. Grind the meat with a ³⁄₁₆- or ⅛-inch wheel. Put the ground meat into a clean bowl and refrigerate for 12 hours.

When you are ready to proceed, divide the meat into two equal loaves. Put each loaf on a flat cookie pan and roll it out into a sheet of ½- to ¼-inch thickness. Cut the sheet with a knife, but do not separate at this point. Place the cookie pans into the center of the oven and dry at 150°F for 4 hours or longer, depending on the thickness of the strips. Cut the strips again to separate them. If need be, turn the strips and dry a little longer. Store in an airtight container in the refrigerator or freezer.

Note: If using a large dehydrator with rectangular plastic trays, you can place the cookie sheets onto the trays. With round units, you'll have to work something out.

Sausage Mix Jerky

Here's a spice mix that I like in country sausage and jerky. Try other sausage spice mixes, but note that the jerky meat should be quite lean, whereas most really good sausage meats contain some fat.

    10 pounds lean red meat
    6 tablespoons salt
    1 tablespoon freshly ground black pepper
    1 tablespoon ground dried red pepper
    ½ tablespoon dried sage

Cut the meat into cubes, spreading them out over a clean work surface. Mix the dry ingredients and sprinkle evenly over the meat. Grind the meat in a sausage mill. Load into a jerky gun and lay some thin ribbons onto dehydrator trays. Dry at 140°F for 6 to 8 hours, or until dry to your liking. This recipe can also be made with the rolling-pin method.

Herbed Jerky

The herbs in this recipe can be changed to suit your taste, but I think it's best to avoid spices like cloves or allspice.

2 pounds ground red meat
1 teaspoon salt
1 teaspoon onion salt
½ teaspoon garlic salt
½ teaspoon lemon-pepper seasoning salt
½ teaspoon dried thyme
½ teaspoon dried oregano
½ teaspoon dried marjoram
½ teaspoon dried basil

Cut the meat into chunks suitable for feeding into the meat grinder and spread them out over a flat surface. Thoroughly mix the rest of the ingredients and sprinkle them evenly on the beef chunks. Grind the beef, using a ³⁄₁₆- or ⅛-inch wheel. Using a jerky shooter, lay the ground beef out in ribbons onto dehydrator trays. Dry at 140°F for 6 to 8 hours, or until dry to your liking.

PART TWO

Beef, Venison, and Other Meats for Jerky

Although most of America's jerky is made from beef these days, many other meats can be used. Some of these are local favorites here and there around the globe. In Tibet, yak jerky is almost a part of the daily diet. In South Africa, both springbok (a large antelope) and ostrich are highly esteemed. In Australia, crocodile jerky is just the ticket. In Europe, these days, due to the mad cow scare, people are leaning toward reindeer from the north country as a more-than-worthy substitute for beef.

In any case, the chapters in part 2 set forth a variety of recipes for culinary sports and jerky aficionados to try, and hopefully the text contains something for everybody. Most of the recipes can be made either in the kitchen oven or in a dehydrator, as well as in the open air, with readily available beef or other good red meat. Before drying a batch, a review of the methods and techniques for using kitchen ovens and dehydrators set forth in part 1 may be helpful. Also remember that many of the recipes in part 1 can also be made with game or other meat as well as with beef. In general, however, venison and other game require less drying time simply because they are leaner and drier meats—just perfect for jerking! Still, many people may find it easier to start with more familiar fare.

6

BEEF: IT'S FOR JERKY

There's no question about it. In spite of modern concerns about its animal fat content, beef is still the favorite meat for jerky in many parts of the world—especially North America, South America, and Australia—partly because it is so readily available. The best or most expensive cuts of beef, however, are not ideal for jerky, simply because they contain lots of fat marbled in the tissue of the meat. (The fat is harder to dry and sometimes reduces storage times.) These expensive cuts come from along the backbone. The front part of the animal, especially the chuck and brisket, is also rather fatty and should be avoided for making jerky if another cut is available. To be sure, fatty beef will make jerky of excellent flavor, but the fat may cause storage problems—and many modern people are trying to cut back on fat. Note also that range-fed animals are not normally as fat as those fed in feedlots, fattened on purpose for the market.

In any case, the best beef for making jerky is lean and contains very little fat marbled in the tissue. For the most part, this meat comes from the hindquarter and the belly or flank. Here's my take:

Flank Steak. Often called London broil, the flank steak is thin, rather like a slab of bacon. It is really the belly muscle of the animal. When trimmed, it weighs about 2½ pounds. The flank steak is quite lean and is rather easily cut into jerky strips, either with the grain or across the grain. Often the flank is cut into smaller steaks and packaged for the meat counter. Ask your butcher for the whole flank, but be warned that some butchers buy beef that has been robbed of the flank steak.

Skirt Steak. This strip of meat—actually diaphragm muscles that control breathing—is a very good choice for making jerky, but these are not always available in supermarkets, because they are sold off to the restaurant trade. Ask your butcher.

Chuck and Brisket. The meat from the chuck or forequarter is usually quite fatty. It can be used for jerky if it is carefully trimmed, but I do not recommend it. In some books, the brisket is recommended for jerky and billed as low in fat. This has not been my experience, and I usually avoid it.

Rib and Loin Meat. The most expensive part of the beef is along the backbone. The meat has a little too much fat marbled in the flesh, making it a poor choice for jerky. If you buy a whole cow, or perhaps a baron, use the loin and tenderloin, as well as the rib eye, for steaks.

Hindquarter. Excellent jerky meat—and lots of it—comes from the hindquarter of the animal. Often the hind leg, or part of it, is cut into round steaks. These have a section of bone in the middle, surrounded by four distinct sections of meat attached by membranes. These sections follow the natural division of the muscles in the leg. Anyone who buys a whole leg or hindquarter of beef, which is what I recommend for those who want to make lots of jerky, can easily reduce it to roasts simply by cutting the meat along the divisions. These roasts can then be cut with the grain into strips, or across the grain into steaks. Invariably there will be odd-shaped chunks and pieces left over. These can be used for stews (along with the bones), sausage, or ground-meat dishes, or you can use them for jerky nuggets and burger jerky, as discussed in chapters 3 and 4. In any case, here are some cuts of meat taken from the hindquarter.

Top Round is the larger of the leg muscles and weighs in at more than 20 pounds. It is lean and has a fine grain—great for jerky.

Bottom Round weighs about 14 pounds. It contains more tough fibers than top round and requires more trimming if you want perfect jerky strips.

Tip Sirloin, known as the silver tip, also weighs about 14 pounds. The meat has a fine texture and makes good jerky, but be warned that the word *sirloin* is often misleading, simply because it is attached as a marketing term to several cuts of meat.

Eye of Round is the smallest muscle in the hind leg, and usually the toughest. It can be cut with the grain into strips or across the grain into small steaks, which in turn can be cut into strips.

Ground Beef. The best meat for grinding comes from the hindquarter, such as top round. The chuck and even the brisket can be used, however, if the meat is carefully trimmed before grinding. Your best bet, if you want to make lots of jerky, is to buy a whole leg or perhaps a whole top round; part of it can be cut into strips or slabs, and the trimmings can be used for grinding. In any case, I do not recommend that off-the-shelf ground meat from supermarkets and other meat outlets be used for making jerky.

The beginner, and some old hands, will probably want to proceed with packaged steaks and other cuts selected from the supermarket. Cut into steaks or cutlets of uniform size and thickness, most of these are certainly easier to cut into strips. Sometimes small steaks are marketed as "breakfast steaks" or some such term. Most of these can be used for making jerky; I have even used packages of stir-fry meat that looked fresh. When making a selection from the packaged meat counter, look for lean red meat, which will not contain specks and spiderwebs of fat. Compare round steak to chuck steak and you'll see the difference.

It's best, always, to buy freshly butchered meats for jerky. Precut packaged meats will have dates on the package, and freshly cut beef will usually have a bright color.

In any case, all of the jerky recipes in part 1 will work with good lean beef. If you like the flavor of beef as much as I do, however, you may want to try a couple of basic recipes, made without a long list of spices and flavorings.

Caveman Jerky

In his book NeanderThin, *Ray Audette sets forth a simple method of making jerky, which could have been made from the wild cattle of the day (aurochs). Simply cut the meat into strips ¼ inch thick and dry it in the sun for a day or two. Audette allows that the oven of a kitchen stove can be used, but adds that a dehydrator is preferable. Use no salt, sugar, or other ingredients.*

10 pounds fresh beef

Put the strips of meat onto the dehydrator trays and dry at 90°F to 100°F for a day or two, or to your liking. Since the jerky contains no salt or other preservatives, it may not keep indefinitely. If practical, store it in a freezer until needed.

A. D.'s Caveman Variation

I have tried Caveman Jerky more than once, and I like it. I do, however, feel a little safer if salt is sprinkled over the meat prior to drying. Besides, salt improves the flavor, costs very little, and gets the juices of the mouth flowing.

10 pounds beef
1 cup salt

Cut the beef into strips about ¼ inch thick. Sprinkle the strips with salt in a nonmetallic container. Toss the meat to coat all sides. Place the strips over the racks of an oven or dehydrator and dry at 140°F for 6 to 8 hours, or until dry to your liking.

Note: To compare this to the no-salt recipe above, separate the meat into two batches and keep it separate for tasting and storing.

A. D.'s Easy Soy Beef Jerky

I've always been fond of meats marinated in a little soy sauce and black pepper. The combination is especially good in jerky. Note, however, that the operative ingredient in soy sauce is salt. I do not recommend the so-called low-salt soy sauce for making jerky unless additional salt is added. Exact measures aren't necessary, but the soy sauce should be enough to coat or wet all sides of the meat. Usually, ½ cup per pound of meat will be about right. Pepper to taste.

    beef strips, ⅛ to ¼ inch thick
    soy sauce
    freshly ground black pepper

Place the beef strips into a nonmetallic container. Pour in a little soy sauce and sprinkle liberally with black pepper. Toss about to coat all sides. Refrigerate overnight. Place the meat strips on a rack in your kitchen oven or dehydrator. Dry at 140°F for 6 to 8 hours, or until the jerky is barely pliable, depending on the exact temperature, humidity, and thickness of the meat. Store in jars, properly sealed, in a cool, dark place, or, better, vacuum-pack in jars or plastic bags. This jerky is especially good when cooked in rice; the soy sauce gives it a Chinese flavor. It also makes a good chew.

Variation: Use red pepper flakes instead of black pepper. Also, try this recipe with half soy sauce and half rice wine or perhaps dry vermouth left over from the martinis.

Thai Fried Jerky

The Thai are fond of a fried beef jerky as a snack, or as part of a complete meal.

2 pounds beef
¼ cup soy sauce
3 tablespoons whole coriander seeds
1½ tablespoons brown sugar
1 tablespoon whole cumin seeds
1–2 cups peanut oil

Roast the coriander and cumin seeds in a cast-iron skillet, bringing out their fragrance. Cool the seeds and grind them with mortar and pestle. Cut the beef into strips ¼ inch thick, 2 inches wide, and 3 inches long, trimming away any fat as you go. Mix the soy sauce, browned seeds, and brown sugar in a nonmetallic container. Add the beef strips and toss to coat all sides. Marinate for an hour or longer. Drain and dry in a kitchen oven or dehydrator for 6 hours, or until the beef is dry to the touch.

Heat the peanut oil in a skillet on medium. Fry the jerky pieces a few at a time until crispy around the edges. Drain on brown bags or absorbent paper. Store in an airtight container at room temperature. Serve alone as a snack or with sticky rice as part of a meal.

Old-Time Dried Beef

If you want a different jerky, try this old recipe from the American National Cow Belles Association. Like many old-time recipes, it calls for saltpeter, which can be omitted entirely, or you can substitute an equal amount of sodium nitrate, available from pharmacists. Note that the recipe calls for large chunks of meat—roasts from 5 to 10 pounds—for a total of 20 pounds. I quote the recipe here mainly for historical interest. Personally, I wouldn't want to try it unless I had a cool, dry place to hang the meat.

"Mix 1 pint of salt, 1 teaspoon saltpeter, and ¼ pound brown sugar. Divide into three parts. Rub into meat for three successive days. Turn beef in the juice formed for 1 week, once each day. Hang in a dry cool place to dry until finished. Put a little extra salt in the holes cut for the cord to hang by. Chunks of beef could be from five to ten pounds in weight. If you like a smoked flavor, smoke the meat after it has quit dripping, then dry. Slice thin when serving."

7

VENISON JERKY

Deer of one sort or another have been hunted for ages. Today, more than thirty species roam wild over much of the world. Almost all species of deer make excellent venison and superior jerky—if they are properly handled. Here's a brief rundown:

White-Tailed Deer. Native to North America, Central America, and parts of South America, the white-tail is currently our most popular big-game animal. In some areas, the population has exploded, causing these animals to be considered pests in many suburban areas and farmlands. In most places, a hunter can take more than one white-tail during the season, buck or doe, in which case the home freezer might well be too full to hold more meat. Jerky is the ideal solution. Note also that frozen venison can be removed from the freezer, thawed, and made into jerky if you need to make room for bumper catches of fish in spring and summer.

Mule Deer. Several subspecies of these animals are native to North and Central America. They make excellent jerky.

Moose. These large animals are called elk in Europe. They also live in Siberia, Mongolia, and Manchuria, as well as in the northern parts of North America. By whatever name, moose make excellent meat and lots of it, as a grown male can weigh up to 1,750 pounds. Jerky strips can be obtained from the saddle, hindquarter, and flank meat.

Elk. This large deer, called *wapiti* by the Native Americans and second in size only to the moose, is a popular game animal in some of the Rocky Mountain states. It also grows in Asia and is raised on farms in Siberia and elsewhere. Weighing in at 1,000 pounds, elk makes excellent jerky and sports very impressive antlers.

Caribou. Also called reindeer, tundra deer, and a dozen other names, these large animals range over the treeless tundra and boreal forests of northern Canada and much of Alaska. The meat—tasty, tender, and very lean—makes excellent jerky. Many of the northernmost Native Americans depend partly on the caribou for sustenance, just as the Lapps do in northern Europe, where the reindeer is more or less domesticated. The meat is available in some American markets and by mail order.

Other Deer. Most other species of deer from around the world also make good jerky, and some, such as the fallow deer from Europe and Asia Minor, are ranched commercially and available in some markets. Some of the world's deer, however, are quite small as compared to the moose or elk. The pudu deer of the Andes, for example, weighs only about 15 pounds. Antelope and other venison-like animals are covered in the next chapter.

• • •

Regardless of the species of deer, the best venison for jerky comes from the loin and the hind leg, saving the shoulders and other parts for boned roasts and stew or burger meat. The loins and tenderloins are relatively easy to reduce to strips or thin slices, cutting the meat with the grain, or cutting it across the grain into medallions, if that shape is acceptable to you. The hind leg, which will have the most meat, is made up of distinct muscles, connected by tissue. If you don't have a meat saw, your best bet is to separate the leg into parts, following the natural division of the meat; then each piece can be reduced to slabs and strips, or perhaps cut across the grain into cutlets of about ½-inch thickness.

If you have a meat saw or use a commercial butcher, another approach would be to cut the whole leg crosswise into thin round steaks. Then remove the center bone and cut the steak into jerky strips. The American Indians had a way of cutting a continuous strip from around the outside of the steak, making a spiral. Having a continuous long strip makes the jerky easy to hang.

Good fresh venison can be jerked to perfection, and the meat doesn't necessarily have to be aged. By "good venison" I mean meat from a deer that was dropped with a well-placed shot instead of being run all over the country—and from a deer that was promptly field-dressed. Such meat has no gamy flavor, unless perhaps it is taken during the rut. If the meat does have a gamy flavor, complicated marinades with a dozen ingredients and secret rubs won't help very much. In any case, a clean kill and prompt field dressing are necessary for good meat, and these essential steps are the hunter's responsibility. I might add that a boar hog or a steer that has been chased all over the country with dogs, shot, slung across the hood of a pickup truck, driven through town for show, and taken to the local meat processor many hours after the kill would probably taste quite "gamy."

Essentially, the field dressing removes the innards from the animal, but it's not the innards as such that cause the so-called gamy flavor. It's the body heat they contain. Thus, field dressing removes much of the total body heat and allows air to circulate in the cavity. Of course, the heat should be removed as soon as possible. (The one exception may be in extremely cold weather.) Removing the heat, and cooling the meat, also makes the venison safer to eat simply because bacteria and such grow best at warm temperature. In this regard, note that the

Department of Agriculture (USDA) has warned that fecal matter can cause *E. coli* contamination in venison. This would probably come from an animal that was not properly field-dressed or was badly gut shot—or, most likely, both. In any event, I don't think the problem is as frequent as regulators would have us believe. If given a choice, I'll take my chances with properly handled venison every time over USDA-inspected chickens or ground meat.

Of course, venison can be purchased in specialized markets these days, as well as by mail or over the Internet. Usually, this meat will be in good shape and will not be gamy. However, beware of venison given away by local hunters. It may be good meat, but the chances are that the hunter is merely passing the buck.

In any case, deer hunters are often people of firm opinion, and many of them have their own ways of jerking venison. Here are a few of my favorites. See also the next chapter, on other large game and exotic meats.

Venison Jerky According to Mel Marshall

Texans are never short on opinions, food-related or otherwise. If Mel Marshall was not a Texan, then he lived in that place long enough to disallow beans in anything called chili. After saying that sun-dried jerky can be made only in places with long, warm summer days and nights and pure, unpolluted air, he added, "Sadly, there is no place today on the North American continent that provides both these conditions." Then he set forth his recipe and alternative method for making it in an oven, pretty much as follows.

    lean venison
    garlic powder
    hickory-smoked salt

Cut the venison into strips about ½ inch thick. Sprinkle the meat with garlic powder and hickory-smoked salt. Arrange the strips on a pan and put into an oven set at its lowest possible temperature (usually 125°F). Dry for 3 to 6 hours (maybe 8 or 10 hours in some ovens), depending on the meat and on the individual oven. Use the jerky as noshing fare, or cook it in soups and stews.

Note that Marshall cuts his meat a little thicker than most experts. This makes it a good chew.

Venison Jerky According to Sam Goolsby

I found this method in The Great Southern Wild Game Cookbook, *by Sam Goolsby, billed on the dust jacket as hunter, outdoor writer, and wild-game expert and pictured in black tie and with shotgun at ready, standing by a white table setting. His recipe for venison jerky requires no oven or dehydrator. He tells us to cut the venison into strips less than ½ inch wide, and I presume that it should be the same thickness or thinner.*

    about 2 pounds venison
    1 gallon boiling water
    1 cup salt
    black pepper and spices of your choice

Cut the venison into strips less than ½ inch wide and less than ½ inch thick. Bring the water to a rolling boil. String the venison strips up on a wire and dip them into the boiling water. As soon as the meat loses its red color, lift it from the water. Drain (but do not rinse) and sprinkle with salt, pepper, and other spices, if desired. Hang the venison in the sun until dry, usually about 2 days. It should be covered during rain and at night. More pepper will help keep the flies away, Goolsby says, if these are a problem. The meat can also be hung in a screened enclosure, but this slows down the drying process, he allows.

Jerked Venison According to Sturdivant

All you need for delicious jerky, sayeth E. N. Sturdivant, author of *Game Cookery,* is fresh venison, salt, pepper, and a sharp knife. Slice the meat with the grain into slabs. Place these on a board and trim away all the fat. Salt and pepper both sides of the meat. Hang the meat on a string or put it on well-ventilated racks, preferably on a screened porch or otherwise protected from flies and insects. With a low humidity and a temperature between 55°F to 70°F, the jerky will be ready in about 2 full days. Remove the jerky and put it into a porous cloth bag. Hang until you are ready to use the jerky.

If you prefer to smoke the jerky, Sturdivant goes on, use a hardwood for smoke, preferably from a nut tree such as hickory or pecan. Build a smoldering fire, with just enough heat to keep the smoke coming. Getting the jerky too hot will make it brittle instead of chewy, he says. After 4 to 6 hours in a smoker, hang the meat as described above to finish the job. "You will find this a highly flavorsome jerky, and quite unlike the kind for sale in stores and delicatessens," he declares. Indeed.

Venison Jerky According to Dr. Longley

Here's a recipe from Dr. Andrew Longley of Cundy's Harbor, Maine, pretty much as published in *The Maine Way,* a collection of fish and game recipes. It calls for cold-smoking, preferably at 80°F, for 12 hours. This recommendation rules the method out for some of us except in winter, but remember that the 80-degree mark is what Dr. Longley considered ideal. (That's a long way from the 160°F recommended by the USDA!)

First, cut the venison into strips as thin as possible, Dr. Longley advises. Lay the strips flat and press them with the flat side of a knife blade until paper-thin. Sprinkle the strips lightly on both sides with salt, then place them in a smoker for 12 hours at 80°F. After smoking, complete the drying by placing the strips uncovered in a frost-free refrigerator. Once dried, the jerky does not have to be refrigerated, he adds.

Deer Jerky According to Don Bangs

A hunter from St. Louis sent this recipe to the Missouri Conservationist in 1954. It eventually found its way into Cy Littlebee's Guide to Cooking Fish & Game, *published by the Missouri Department of Conservation, on which this account was based. The curing mix is made ahead of the hunt and will be enough to jerk a hindquarter.*

FOR THE CURE MIX:

   3 pounds salt
   ½ cup black peppercorns
   ¼ cup allspice berries (whole)

Grind the peppercorns and allspice berries, using a spice mill or perhaps mortar and pestle. Mix together with the salt. Set aside or store in a jar until needed.

FOR THE JERKY:

Dress the deer as soon as possible after the kill. Debone the hind leg, separating the muscles by their natural division. Trim off the membranes. Ideally, the pieces should be 4 inches thick, 6 to 8 inches wide, and no longer than 12 inches. (Trimmings can be used for stew meat.) Rub the curing powder onto the surface of the meat, evenly and thoroughly. Attach a string to the small end of each piece of meat and hang it in the wind. If the sun is hot, hang the meat in the shade. (In the North, Bangs adds, the sun helps the process.) If the weather is rainy, hang the meat near the campfire, but do not expose it to more smoke than necessary. Cover the meat with canvas at night and during a rain. "Meat prepared like this is not at its best until it's about a month old. After that no hunter or trapper can get enough," he says.

I recommend using the meat in soups and stews that will be simmered for several hours.

20-Gauge Venison Jerky

I asked Chef Myron Becker, a culinary sport who brews and markets the 20-Gauge Wild Game Sauce, whether he had a jerky recipe for me to try. He replied that his friend and fishing buddy, Don Chapin of Cape Cod, has made copious amounts of venison jerky using 20-Gauge in a marinade application. "He just tossed the strips in a ziplock bag with a bit more than enough 20-Gauge to coat them well, squeezed out all of the air, zipped it up, and let them sit overnight in the refrigerator. The next morning he put the strips into a drying oven. He also tried just a salt-and-pepper cure and then brushed the 20-Gauge onto the strips while in the drying oven. I thought the marinaded version was better. Sometimes he finished the jerky in a smoker with a light applewood- or grapevine-smoked finish."

Alaskan Venison Jerky

Here's a good jerky recipe that I used in my book Complete Fish & Game Cookbook, *as adapted from an article by Karen Cantillion in* Alaska Fish

& Game *magazine. The venison should be cut into strips about 1 inch wide and ¼ inch thick. For a brittle texture, cut the meat across the grain; for a chewy texture, cut the meat with the grain. I normally use the muscles from the hind leg. The meat should be fat-free and well trimmed. Make sure that the soy sauce is not salt-free; if it is, add some salt to the recipe.*

    3 pounds venison strips
    ½ cup Worcestershire sauce
    ½ cup soy sauce
    1 tablespoon Liquid Smoke
    1 tablespoon onion powder
    1 tablespoon garlic powder
    1 tablespoon black pepper
    red pepper flakes to taste
    Tabasco sauce to taste

Mix all the ingredients except the meat. Put the meat into a non-metallic container and pour the marinade over it, tossing well to cover all surfaces of the meat. Marinate in the refrigerator for 8 to 12 hours. Drain the meat and put it on racks in your oven, placing a shallow baking pan at the bottom to catch any drippings. Turn the oven to 150°F for 6 to 8 hours, or until the meat is dry. Leave the oven door ajar so that the moisture can escape. (A dehydrator can also be used.) Store the jerky in tightly covered containers. Refrigeration isn't necessary.

Hickory-Smoked Whitetail Jerky

This recipe was submitted by J. Oscar Sullivan to The South Carolina Wildlife Cookbook, *first published in rather scant detail by the South Carolina Wildlife and Marine Resources Department.*

venison
salt and pepper
hickory chips

Cut the venison into strips from ¼ to ⅜ inch thick. Rub both sides with salt and pepper. Hang the strips in a cool place until they are dry and stiff. Then smoke with hickory chips. Store in a jar. "This always used to be in the pantry and was our 'candy' in the old days," Sullivan said.

A. D.'s Sea Salt Jerky

I like this jerky made with sea salt. Ordinary table salt can also be used.

2 pounds venison
1 cup sea salt
½ gallon spring water

Dissolve the salt in the water in a nonmetallic container. Cut the venison into strips about ¼ inch thick. Place the venison strips into the brine and stir about with a wooden spoon. Cover and refrigerate overnight. Drain the strips and arrange them on the racks of your oven or dehydrator trays. Dry at 145°F for 6 to 8 hours, or until dry to your liking. Cool the strips and store in a cloth bag or in vacuum-packed Mason jars, depending partly on how long you intend to keep the jerky.

Sylvia Bashline's Spicy Venison Jerky

Here's a good venison jerky recipe adapted from The Bounty of the Earth Cookbook, *by Sylvia Bashline. She says the jerky will store for*

many months, but warns that it will surely be gobbled up before it has a chance to get cold! I agree.

> 1 ½ pounds venison round steak
> ¼ cup soy sauce
> 3 tablespoons steak sauce
> 1 teaspoon onion powder
> 1 teaspoon celery seeds
> 1 teaspoon seasoned salt
> ¼ teaspoon black pepper

Partly freeze the venison steak, then cut it into thin strips. Thoroughly mix the rest of the ingredients. Put the meat into a plastic bag, pour in the marinade, and place in the refrigerator overnight, turning the bag a time or two. Drain the venison strips on paper towels. Dry on oven racks at 150°F until the moisture is gone. Store in a covered container.

Wyoming Jerked Elk

Many of the old-time recipes call for a small amount of saltpeter (see also appendix A, "Jerky Ingredients and Safety"). The stuff can be purchased at the pharmacy, or it can be omitted. If you use it in this recipe, mix it thoroughly into the brown sugar solution. If you follow the drying procedure for this one, you'll need cotton twine and dry weather.

> 4 pounds lean elk
> 1 cup salt
> 1 cup brown sugar
> 1 tablespoon crushed allspice
> ½ tablespoon red pepper flakes

½ tablespoon saltpeter
water

Cut the meat into slices ¼ inch thick. Make a layer in a nonmetallic container. Sprinkle with salt. Repeat until all the meat is layered, using all the salt. Dissolve the brown sugar in water. Stir in the saltpeter, allspice, and red pepper. Mix thoroughly. Pour the mixture over the layered meat. Marinate for 36 hours. Using a darning needle, tie a loop of cotton twine on the end of each strip of meat. Hang the strips on a wire or clothesline, using clothespins to secure the twine to the main line. The jerky will dry in a few days, depending on the weather. It's best to bring it inside at night or during a rain.

Honey-Mustard Jerky

This recipe works with any good lean meat. Try it with elk or other game. Cut the meat into strips about 1 inch wide, 6 inches long, and ¼ inch thick, with or against the grain, depending on how the jerky will be used. Try some both ways.

5 pounds lean venison
2½ cups soy sauce
½ cup honey
2 tablespoons prepared mustard
2 tablespoons onion juice
1 tablespoon salt

Mix the liquid ingredients and salt. Put the meat into a nonmetallic container, cover with the liquid mixture, and toss to cover all sides. Marinate for several hours. Drain and dry in the oven or in a dehydrator at 145°F for about 6 to 8 hours, or until done to your liking.

Moose Jerky

Here's a good recipe for moose, which, according to some culinary sports, makes the best possible jerky. The meat should be from the hind leg, trimmed and cut into strips about ¼ inch thick or a little thinner.

2 pounds moose meat
2 cups soy sauce
¼ cup honey
1 tablespoon prepared mustard
1 teaspoon onion salt
1 teaspoon garlic salt

Mix all the ingredients except the meat in a nonmetallic container. Add the meat, tossing about to coat all sides. Cover the container and refrigerate for 8 hours or overnight, turning the meat a time or two. Drain the meat and arrange the strips on dehydrator trays or oven racks. Dry at 140°F for 6 to 8 hours, or until dry to your liking.

Two-Pepper Moose Jerky

This recipe makes a rather hot jerky from moose or other good lean meat. Increase or decrease the pepper measures to taste.

2 pounds moose, cut into strips ¼ inch thick
1 cup soy sauce
1 cup beer

1 tablespoon red pepper flakes
1 tablespoon freshly ground black pepper
1 tablespoon garlic salt
1 teaspoon Liquid Smoke

Mix all the ingredients except the meat in a nonmetallic container. Add the meat strips, toss about to coat all sides, cover, and refrigerate overnight. Drain the jerky and dry the strips at 140°F for 6 to 8 hours, or longer.

Lemon-Pepper Mule Deer Jerky

Mule deer makes excellent jerky. It's best to use meat from the hind leg, either cut into steaks or separated into roasts. Cut the meat into strips about ¼ inch thick.

2 pounds mule deer
1 cup soy sauce
lemon-pepper seasoning salt
garlic powder

Put the meat strips into a nonmetallic container and pour the soy sauce over them. Toss the meat about to coat all sides. Remove and drain the meat, discarding any remaining soy sauce. Sprinkle both sides of the meat with garlic powder and lemon-pepper seasoning salt. Place the strips on oven racks and dry at 140°F for 6 to 8 hours or longer, depending on how dry you want the jerky. Cool and store in an airtight container, preferably vacuum-packed.

8

OTHER DOMESTIC, GAME, AND EXOTIC MEAT JERKY

Most big-game species make excellent jerky if they are properly field-dressed, and several large animals are now ranched commercially either for meat or for hunting, or both. Sometimes this is merely a matter of managing wild herds, and sometimes it involved stocking exotic species from another land.

Almost all of these farmed or managed animals have been hunted at one time or another in the wild. The giraffe, for instance, has excellent meat and can weigh up to 2 tons. They were once pursued on horseback in Africa for sport as well as for meat. Today the giraffe fits a niche on some small farms and pasturelands that have a few shade trees suitable for long-necked animals (up to 18 feet high) to browse on. Giraffe meat is highly esteemed, and the bone marrow is considered a delicacy in Africa. Other examples include the capybara, a wetland rodent (weighing up to 140 pounds) that is actually hunted and rounded up on horseback in Venezuela.

Some of these meats are readily available in specialized markets and by Internet or mail order. The bison or American buffalo is surely among the best of these meats—and might well be better than beef (see the recipe later in this chapter). The farm-raised ostrich and emu are also gaining in popularity, along with the smaller rhea, but these are covered in the chapter on birds.

If you dress your won game or exotics from the farm, be warned that proper handling is necessary. This includes prompt field dressing, as discussed in chapter 7. Notes on the various meats are set forth under the headings below and in the recipes that appear later in this chapter.

Before getting into exotics, however, we'll take a quick look at more common fare.

Pork. Since pork can carry the parasite that causes trichinosis in humans, it is not a good choice for making jerky. Note that most jerky is not really cooked, and tons of it are made at marginal temperatures that are not carefully controlled. In short, I don't feel good about eating pork jerky, and I am not going to recommend it to others. Some people maintain that freezing the meat at 0°F or lower for twenty-one days will kill the parasites, but it doesn't completely eliminate the idea, at least not in my mind. Still, fresh pork can make excellent jerky, at least in taste. If you want to try it, choose the loin or meat from the hind leg, which won't be as fatty as the typical shoulder (which includes the picnic ham and Boston butt).

Sheep or Lamb. Sheep and lamb are very important in some parts of the world, and they make excellent jerky. It's best to buy a hind leg and reduce it to pieces, following the natural division of the muscles. These can then be cut into long strips. Or have your butcher cut the leg into 1-inch steaks. These can then be easily sliced into strips.

Antelope. There are several kinds of wild antelope, and some are ranched more or less commercially. In South Africa, springbok jerky, or *biltong*, is highly esteemed. In general, follow the directions for deer in chapter 7.

Bison and Buffalo. The American bison, commonly called buffalo, might well be the best of all red meats. Lean, red, and sweet, it makes purely excellent jerky. The bison was hunted almost to extinction during the country's westward expansion, but these days it is ranched commercially, and limited hunting may be available. The real buffalo of Africa and Asia also produces good meat suitable for jerky; studies have been made on the feasibility of raising these animals commercially in the swampy lands of Florida and other places.

Wild Boar and Pigs. These are not recommended for jerky because, like domestic hogs and bears, they carry the parasite that causes trichinosis in humans. I think they are safer than supermarket pork, but many other people and government officials in charge of inspecting the nation's meats will disagree.

Mountain Goat and Sheep. These animals have surprisingly mild meat, for the most part, but old ones are likely to be quite tough. Strips of jerky can be cut out of the hind leg quarter, and any of the meat can be cut into jerky nuggets or ground for use with a jerky gun.

Bear. Although the flesh of a young but fully grown bear is one of the very best of meats, and although bear fat is used in some areas for pastry making and frying foods, it should not be used for jerky. The culprit is the parasite that causes trichinosis. Like pork, bear meat should be cooked well done—to an internal temperature of 165°F to 170°F. In Russia, however, where the meat is highly prized, bear hams are often dry-cured and eaten raw, thinly sliced like prosciutto.

Lion, Bobcats, Lynx, and Other Cats. Excellent meat, mild and lean. Ernest Hemingway gives us a recipe for grilled loin of African lion, which he and his wife, Mary, sampled raw during the field-dressing operation. ("We both thought the clean pink flesh delicious, steak tartare without the capers," Mary later recounted.) Mountain lion or cougar also has lean, mild, white meat, and the smaller wild cats, such as lynx, were highly prized by Native

Americans and early settlers. Check the game laws, however, before shooting any of these big cats. Wild-food guru Euell Gibbons once ate a bobcat, reporting that the "bob" part was quite tasty but the "cat" part was hard to swallow. I feel pretty much the same way about jerky made from anything with *cat* in the name, except, of course, for catfish.

Beaver. In many areas, beavers are so plentiful that some consider them to be pests, free for the taking. The meat is very good, and sometimes trappers will have it in great plenty. Jerky strips can be cut from the hind leg and loin, and the rest provides ground meat or jerky nuggets.

Rabbit and Hare. These small-game animals are often available to the hunter, and some states have very liberal game laws for them. In Florida, for example, there is no closed season or limit restrictions on rabbits, which include the cottontail, the large swamp rabbit (a hare), and the smaller marsh rabbit. Most of these are small and difficult to cut into jerky strips, except possibly for the backstrap (loin) that runs along either side of the backbone, but the meat can be cut into nuggets or ground. The snowshoe hare weighs 3 pounds or better, and the much larger tundra hare can weigh in at 15 pounds. All rabbits should be field-dressed promptly. If properly handled, the meat is mild and lean. Of course, domestic rabbits raised for food can also be used for jerky.

Kangaroo and Other Bush Meats. Several animals from Australia make good jerky. Some imported animals, such as the rabbit, the buffalo, and the camel, are also available as bush meat. Some of these meats, as well as prepared jerky, can be purchased by mail order and over the Internet.

Alligator and Crocodile. Excellent meat, lean and white. Once considered endangered, the alligator has made a remarkable comeback in some of the lower southern states, some of which offer limited hunting. The meat is also available from alligator farms and dealers who traffic in exotic meats. Here in Florida where I live, I can buy all I want from legal sources: They process animals taken by licensed hunters who go after nuisance 'gators, which sometimes take a liking to backyard pools and golf course ponds. The American crocodile, which lives in the brackish waters on the fringes of the Everglades, is still endangered and highly protected. Crocodile meat, and prepared jerky, is available from Australia and perhaps other countries. Also, several cousins of alligators and crocodiles grow in various parts of the world, mostly tropical. All make good eating. See the recipe below.

• • •

Clearly, most edible animals make good jerky, if they are properly handled. Here are some favorite recipes.

Buffalo Jerky

The American Plains Indians depended on jerky made from buffalo. It was the only way they had to preserve the meat; jerking the meat also made it much easier to transport from one camp to another. As a rule, they merely hung the meat out in the sun to dry, or perhaps strung it inside the tepee during rainy weather. A smoky fire was used if necessary to help dry the jerky and to keep away the bugs—but often the fuel (buffalo chips) did not much improve the flavor. Actually, the flavor of rich sweet meat from a prime animal properly dressed needs no enhancement, but I do insist on a little salt, partly for flavor, partly to help draw out the moisture, and partly to help preserve the meat.

The best meat for jerky comes from the hindquarter, with the cuts being similar to beef.

buffalo meat, cut into ¼-inch strips
salt

Sprinkle the buffalo strips heavily with salt and keep in a nonmetallic container overnight, turning them a time or two. Rinse the meat in fresh water, pat dry with paper towels, and arrange the strips on oven or dehydrator trays. Dry at 140°F for 6 to 8 hours, or longer.

Note: If you have good sun in a dry climate without many flies swarming about, try hanging the strips out during the day, exposed to the sunlight. If need be, finish the job in a dehydrator after sunset.

Varmint Jerky

Here's a recipe from the great state of Louisiana, where nutria have become something of a pest in some wetlands. The recipe is said to work with both muskrat and nutria, as well as beef and venison. I have used it with large swamp rabbit, and I wouldn't hesitate to try it with woodchuck. It's best to slice the meat to a thickness of ¼ inch, adjusting the width and length to the size and shape of the meat. If you end up with odd chunks of meat, save them for a stew or perhaps jerk them for use as stew meat. Trim away any fat and gristle. Make sure that the soy sauce is not the low-salt kind; if it is, add some salt.

3 pounds nutria
1 cup brown sugar
1 cup soy sauce
⅔ cup Worcestershire sauce
6 tablespoons Liquid Smoke
1 tablespoon onion powder
1 tablespoon garlic powder
1 teaspoon black pepper

Mix all the ingredients except the meat in a nonmetallic container. Add the meat, tossing about to coat all sides. Cover and refrigerate overnight, stirring a time or two with a wooden spoon. The next morning, pat the meat dry with paper towels, then distribute the strips on dehydrator trays. Dry at 250°F for several hours, or until the jerky is dry to your liking.

Note: I would prefer my jerky to be prepared at 140°F or lower, but 250°F is what this recipe recommends. Suit yourself.

Alligator and Crocodile Jerky

Both alligator and crocodile make excellent jerky. In spite of the popularity of the term alligator tail steaks, some of the best meat comes from the front and hind legs and from along the backbone. The leg meat, however, is difficult to cut into long strips. Your best bet is to use a segment of the loin or tenderloin, or make chunk jerky from the legs.

Any good jerky recipe can be used for these meats, but I would suggest a marinade that won't greatly discolor the nice white meat, as in the following.

2 pounds alligator meat, cut into ¼-inch strips
1 quart spring water
½ cup sea salt
½ cup lemon juice

Mix all the ingredients in a nonmetallic bowl. Refrigerate overnight. Drain the meat and arrange the strips on trays for the dehydrator or kitchen oven. Dry at 140°F for 6 to 7 hours or so. Most of this will be eaten right away. If you want to save some for future use, dry it a little longer and store it in airtight jars, preferably vacuum-packed.

Alaskan Big-Batch Wild-Game Jerky

Here's a recipe for jerking large batches of meat from moose, elk, caribou, or other game when freezing the meat might be a problem, either because of remote location or because the home freezer is full. You'll need some large crockery pickle vats to hold the salt cure and the meat, but plastic containers will do, if necessary. Do not use metal.

> 50 pounds meat, cut into strips ¼–½ inch thick
> 2 gallons soy sauce
> 3 pounds brown sugar
> 1½ pounds chopped fresh garlic or wild onions
> 4 ounces black pepper
> 8 ounces saltpeter
> 6 gallons spring water

Heat the water and add all the ingredients except the meat. Let the brine cool. Add the meat, cover, and let cure for 5 or 6 days in a cool place, stirring with a wooden paddle a time or two daily. Rinse the meat in fresh water. Air-dry the meat strips for an hour or so, then arrange them on dehydrator trays. Dry for 6 to 8 hours at 140°F. If you can't dry the whole batch at one time, start drying it after 4 days in the cure. Process in batches until you finish. Dry this jerky thoroughly and store in vacuum-packed bags or Mason jars until needed.

Jamaican Goat Jerky

Goats are popular in parts of the West Indies, Mexico, and points south, and jerky from the goats of Jamaica, dried in the mountain air, was once an important food for way-stopping mariners. Here's a recipe calling for jerk seasoning, which is popular in Jamaica in both dry and wet form. There are many formulas, but all good jerk contains lots of allspice berries (native to the island), very hot bird or habañero peppers, garlic, onions, and salt. Dry jerk seasoning is available in most spice markets, in some supermarkets, and by mail order. Most jerk seasoning is quite hot, so use it sparingly in your first batch of Jamaican jerky.

Goat meat is available in some places, and often farmers will sell one on the hoof. It's best to use a young one. The meat can be cut into neat strips, small chunks, and various pieces, every which way.

I have always wanted to explore the etymological connection, if any, between jerky and jerk seasoning—but I promise not to do so here.

goat meat
jerk seasoning
dark rum
freshly ground sea salt and black pepper

Roll the meat in a little rum and set it aside for 30 minutes or so. Then sprinkle it with the jerk seasoning, along with a little freshly ground sea salt and black pepper. Dry in a slow oven or dehydrator.

9

BIRD JERKY

Most edible birds make good jerky, but the meat on the smaller birds doesn't lend itself to long strips. Usually the breast is your best bet for most bird jerky—but this isn't always the case. Some of the very large birds, such as the ostrich, have the better meat in the thigh. In any case, these large birds are the easiest to use. For variety and flavor, however, the hunter has the best choices, partly because a wild turkey is better than a domesticated bird. The next best choice is enjoyed by the farmer or those who raise their own chickens and turkeys and other birds for the table. The worst choice comes from the modern poultry "farm" and the supermarket, owing partly to salmonella problems associated with mass production, mass distribution, and mass marketing.

Big Flightless Birds

Several species of large, flightless birds have evolved down through the ages. The ones that have survived modern hunters are swift runners, and even these are no match for the modern long-range rifle rigged with telescopic sights. Among the survivors are the ostrich of Africa, the emu of Australia, and the rhea of South America—all of which were once hunted for food and sport, and are now being raised commercially on farms in North America and other parts of the world. At present, the meat is more expensive than beef or pork, at least in this country, but the price may come down as it becomes more widely available. The meat is currently sold in specialty meat markets, by mail order, and in a few upscale supermarkets.

In any case, these are large flightless birds with lean, dark cherry-red meat. In taste the meat compares readily to beef, but it is sweeter. The meat has much less fat and cholesterol than beef, and it is lower in calories than chicken or turkey. The birds do have fat, but it is not marbled in the grain of the meat.

The ostrich is the largest ratite, weighing as much as 400 pounds. The emu is much smaller, about 140 pounds, and the rhea weighs in at less than 100 pounds. The best meat on all of these birds is on the thigh, not the breast, which is rather flat. Market forms include steaks (usually thigh meat), fillets, roasts, ground meat, and so on. Some firms that specialize in these birds may have whole birds or halves for sale, or perhaps leg and thigh quarters.

Aussie Bush Jerky

The emu still grows wild in Australia, where it was once hunted with boomerangs, but it is also raised commercially in the United States and Canada. Be sure to try it.

3 pounds emu thigh meat
1 cup pineapple juice
¾ cup soy sauce
¼ cup salt
¼ cup brown sugar
3 cloves garlic, crushed
2 tablespoons finely grated fresh gingerroot
1 tablespoon black pepper
½ teaspoon cayenne pepper

Cut the emu meat into strips about ⅜ inch thick. Mix the rest of the ingredients in a nonmetallic container, stirring well. Add the meat strips, toss about to coat all sides, and marinate for 8 hours. Drain the meat and pat it dry with paper towels or cloth. Arrange the strips on dehydrator trays (or oven racks) and dry it at 145°F for 2 hours. Reduce the heat to 130°F for about 6 hours, or until the jerky is as dry as you want it.

Note: This recipe can also be used with ostrich, rhea, and other good red meats.

Bush *Biltong*

Ostrich meat was highly esteemed by the ancient Roman epicures, and wild ostrich was once hunted extensively in Africa. Since they have very keen eyesight and can run 40 miles per hour, they were worthy game for the bushman armed with primitive weapons. Now farmed commercially in Africa, North America, France, and other parts of the world, the ostrich makes a very good jerky. Most of the recipes for red meat can be used for ostrich, but here's the real biltong, made with rather thick strips of meat. Don't try this one unless you have a cool, dry climate.

> ostrich thigh meat
> salt
> vinegar

Cut the meat into strips about 2 inches wide and 1 inch thick. Sprinkle both sides with salt, rubbing it in well. Put the meat into a nonmetallic container and leave it overnight. Dip a clean rag in vinegar, wring it out, and wipe off the strips of meat. Hang the strips in a cool, dry, airy place until dry.

Variation: Use a dehydrator on the lowest heat setting, in which case drying may take 2 days or longer. If you are in a hurry, use thinner strips and dry it in a dehydrator at 140°F for 6 to 8 hours, or until dry to your liking.

Rhea Jerky

Once hunted with the bola, these birds still roam the grassy plains of Argentina. They are also farmed commercially in North America and abroad. As compared to most peoples of South America, the Argentines don't spice their food highly. The strips of meat are best cut from "round" steaks taken from the thigh.

> 2 pounds rhea thigh meat, cut into thin strips
> sea salt

Salt the strips of meat heavily on both sides. Put the strips into a nonmetallic container, cover, and refrigerate overnight, turning a time or two if convenient. Rinse the strips, pat dry, and arrange on dehydrator or oven trays. Dry at 140°F for 6 to 8 hours, or until it is done to your liking. This jerky can be eaten as is, or it can be used in cooking, as is the custom in much of South America.

See also *Charqui* Mendoza, page 41.

TURKEY, CHICKEN, AND GUINEA FOWL

Turkey breast is usually your best bet for jerky, simply because there's lots of it. When partly frozen, the meat can be cut lengthwise into strips or across the grain for medallions. It's best, of course, to bone the meat before jerking.

Chicken is much smaller but the principle is the same. One possibility is to use frozen "chicken tender" pieces, those choice strips of meat found in the innermost part of the breast. These are available in 10-pound bags from wholesale outfits that sell food in fairly large lots.

Guinea fowl, also called guinea hens and African pheasants, are game birds in West Africa and are raised commercially in some parts of the world. In the American South, they are a popular barnyard bird. The meat is lean and quite tasty.

Ducks and Geese

Both geese and domestic ducks have lots of fat, but most of it is under the skin. The meat itself is lean and tasty. Wild ducks and wild geese may or may not have lots of fat, depending on what they have been eating. The diet also determines the taste. In general, fish-eating ducks have a strong flavor and are not recommended for jerky, unless perchance you have a taste for Thai fish sauce.

In both ducks and geese, the easiest and best jerky comes from the breast, which is simply filleted on both sides, leaving a slab of meat. The whole slab can be dried, or it can be cut into strips for regular jerky. In either case, the fine-grained lean meat makes an excellent chew. If you want to use the whole bird, trim away the fat and cut it into chunks for jerky nuggets or grind it for ground-meat jerky. Personally, I prefer to jerk the breast and use the rest of the bird for duck soup.

Duck Breast Jerky

Make this jerky with whole duck breast fillets, skinned and trimmed—but not sliced. Use either wild ducks, large or small, or domestic birds, but adjust the drying times as necessary. The recommendations below are for mallard-size birds.

    duck breasts, boned and skinned
    hickory-smoked salt
    brown sugar
    salt and pepper

Mix the hickory-smoked salt, brown sugar, salt, and black pepper. Sprinkle the duck breast fillets liberally on both sides and layer in a nonmetallic container. Cover and chill for 2 days, turning several times. Pat the fillets dry with absorbent paper and place them in a single layer on a baking sheet or dehydrator tray. Sprinkle again with the seasoning mix. Dry at 140°F for 6 to 8 hours, or until dry but still bendable without breaking. Cool and slice either across the grain or with the grain, depending on whether you want to chew the jerky as is or use it in recipes.

UPLAND GAME BIRDS

Most game birds, such as quail and dove, are too small to be practical for making jerky. The pheasant has lean, white meat and can be used to advantage. The real prize, at least in North America, is the wild turkey. It can be used like domestic turkey—and really is better meat. Some other birds, such as sandhill crane, can be hunted on a limited basis in some areas.

Pheasant Breast Jerky

Almost any good jerky recipe can be used for pheasant breast, but I think a teriyaki marinade works just right. Do not use a no-salt mixture, however, unless you add some salt to the marinade.

pheasant breasts, cut into strips about ⅜ inch thick
commercial teriyaki sauce
sake, sherry, or dry vermouth

Put the pheasant strips into a nonmetallic container. Add a little teriyaki sauce and sake. Toss about to coat all sides. Marinate in the refrigerator for several hours. Arrange the strips on dehydrator trays and dry at 140°F for 6 hours, or until done to your liking.

10

FISH JERKY

Tasty jerky can be made from a variety of fresh- and saltwater fish. As a rule, those fish with firm, white, low-fat flesh will dry and store better (or longer) than fatty species. Some rather fatty species, such as salmon, can be used, however, and are in fact often recommended for jerky, possibly because the fillets are boneless, easy to slice into strips, and readily available in fish markets.

Personally, I put more stock in freshness than in species, and I really do prefer to catch and dress my own fish for jerking. Fresh fish can be purchased at the market, if you have a trained eye and a good nose or trust your fishmonger. Look for fish with bright eyes.

There is nothing wrong with making jerky from properly frozen fish—if they were frozen while very fresh. I like frozen grouper fillets, for example, from the Gulf of Mexico. People who catch their own fish should gut them and put them on ice as soon as possible. The larger the fish, as a rule, the more important this rule becomes. A shark, for example, might well have dozens of pounds of excellent meat if it is gutted and iced as soon as it is caught. Within minutes in the hot sunlight, however, the flesh of some sharks develops uric acid and smells like ammonia.

I am reluctant to set forth a list of fish suitable for making jerky, partly because there is so much confusion in the fish trade and in sport fishermen's lingo. *Catfish*, for example, can refer to many things, ranging from a barely edible bullhead to a choice channel cat from a clean river, so that recommending catfish in general would be very misleading, or could be. There are dozens if not hundreds of other problem fish. *Bass* can mean many things. Or *perch*. The perch that some writers and chefs have in mind is the ocean perch, a fish that is quite fatty, whereas the perch that some freshwater anglers have in mind is the white perch or yellow perch, both of which have lean flesh. Also note that some so-called trash fish make excellent jerky.

In general, however, I will say that fillets from large fish work better than those for small ones, simply because they are easier to cut into jerky strips. Also, the bellies of large fish often provide convenient jerky meat, because they are rather flat and of a uniform thickness, making them easy to slice, just as bacon is sliced from a slab of sow belly.

Salmon Jerky

Native Americans, the Japanese Ainu, and other peoples just below the fringes of the Arctic Circle have enjoyed salmon in great plenty during the spring spawning run upstream. Drying the fish was the best way to preserve it for consumption throughout the year. If we reduce the salmon to boneless strips of meat before drying it, we've got jerky. The strips, of course, are easily obtained by cutting the boneless fillets crosswise or perhaps on a diagonal to a uniform width. I prefer to leave the skin on, but skinless fillets can also be used. In any case, this simple jerky can be prepared in a small electric smoker on the patio.

5 pounds boneless salmon fillets
1 cup fine sea salt
1 gallon spring water
green wood for smoking

Cut the fillets into strips from ½ to ¾ inch thick. Dissolve the salt into the water in a nonmetallic container. Mix in the salmon strips. Place a clean plate on top to hold all the salmon strips under the water. Refrigerate for 12 hours or longer. Remove the strips and rinse in fresh water, preferably running, for about an hour to remove the excess salt. Place the strips on racks and allow to dry in the air for 3 or 4 hours. They will dry quicker if placed in a breeze or under a fan.

Rig for smoking at 145°F. Place some green-wood chips around the coals or heat. Place the strips in the smoker for 6 to 8 hours, more or less, depending on the heat and the thickness of the meat. When ready, the jerky will be dry and firm to the touch, but will not crumble. Take a test bite. It should be chewy. Cool the jerky and then store it in airtight containers. I prefer to vacuum-pack mine in Mason jars. Store in a cool place for up to 3 months.

Variation: Try this recipe without the smoke. In step 2, use a dehydrator or kitchen oven.

Cheyenne's Marinated Salmon Jerky

Here's a good recipe that I received from Cheyenne West, who once published a magazine about cooking fish and game and wild stuff. The combination of honey, rum, and lemon juice goes nicely with salmon. Note that the recipe does not contain much salt or such salty ingredients as soy sauce. Hence, I don't recommend the recipe for long storage. Not to worry, though: It's so good that a pound won't last very long.

    1-pound salmon fillet
    ¼ cup honey
    ¼ cup rum
    juice of 1 lemon
    5 allspice berries

5 whole cloves
5 crushed peppercorns
1 teaspoon garlic salt
½ teaspoon dried parsley
1 bay leaf

Slice the fillet into strips about ⅜ inch thick. Mix all the ingredients except the fish in a nonmetallic container. Let sit for 15 minutes or longer. Add the salmon strips one at a time. Cover and refrigerate for 1 hour, turning the strips a few times as convenient. Arrange the strips on trays or racks and dry for 6 to 8 hours at 140°F, or until dry to your liking. Store each strip separately in a ziplock bag, Cheyenne says.

Shark Jerky

This jerky recipe is based on information distributed by the California Sea Grant, the University of California, and the U.S. Department of Agriculture. The Sea Grant people recommend using blue shark, but any good shark will work. There are dozens of edible species—blacktip, spinner, soupfin, mako, lemon, leopard, and so on—but in many cases the fish must be gutted and iced down as soon as it is boated or landed.

The procedure that follows, adapted from my *Saltwater Fish Cookbook,* is for making the jerky in a kitchen oven. It works just as well using a commercial dehydrator.

Start with about 3 pounds of shark fillets. Cut the fillets into strips of convenient length, ½ to ¾ inch thick and 2 inches wide. You can cut with or against the grain, thereby producing a different texture in the final product. Cutting with the grain will produce a chewier jerky. Note that partly frozen shark is much easier to slice.

Prepare a sauce with ⅛ cup of teriyaki sauce, ⅛ cup of Liquid Smoke, and 6 drops of Tabasco sauce.

Place the shark strips on racks. Sprinkle moderately with onion salt, garlic salt, and table salt. Turn the strips and sprinkle the other side.

Mix the shark strips and the sauce thoroughly in a large plastic bag. Expel the air from the bag and seal. (Use a vacuum-seal system if available.)

Marinate for 12 hours in the refrigerator, turning the bag a time or two.

Remove the shark strips and place them on the oven racks.

Turn the oven to 140°F. Leave the door ajar. Start checking the jerky after 2 or 3 hours, but leave it in the oven until firm, dry, and tough—but not crumbly. It should be rather rubbery. The curing time will vary, and may take as long as 12 hours. A good deal depends on the thickness of the meat, individual ovens (and thermostatic controls), and sometimes on the species of shark.

Store the strips in airtight jars in a cool place. Enjoy.

Halibut Popcorn

Here's an interesting recipe adapted from the excellent book Cooking Alaskan. *To make it you will need a long, thin, very sharp knife. The recipe calls for halibut fillet, which can be quite a chunk of meat from a large fish.*

halibut fillet
salt in a large shaker

Skin the fillet and slice it very thin—thin enough to see the knife blade through the fish flesh. Salt each strip heavily on both sides and hang to air-dry. The dried strips will taste "quite a bit like popcorn," the book says—but they really don't.

Spicy Fish Jerky

Use this recipe with boneless fillets of any mild fish, preferably low in fat content. The strips can be cut across the grain, on a bias, or lengthwise.

2 pounds fish strips
½ cup tomato sauce
2 tablespoons minced onion
1 tablespoon minced garlic
1 tablespoon salt
1 tablespoon cayenne pepper
1 tablespoon freshly ground black pepper
1 tablespoon dried thyme
1 tablespoon dried basil
1 tablespoon Liquid Smoke

Mix all the ingredients except the fish in a nonmetallic container. Let stand for 15 minutes. Add the fish one strip at a time, gently tossing about to coat all sides. Marinate for an hour or two, turning a time or two. Drain the fish strips and place on a dehydrator tray or fine-mesh oven rack. Dry at 140°F for 6 to 8 hours, or until done to your liking. This jerky can be stored for a few days in an airtight container, preferably vacuum-packed.

Catfish Jerky

Some catfish make an excellent jerky, but there are so many edible species and so much prejudice and misunderstanding about the genre that it's difficult to hold this text to a reasonable length. In general, the better the meat, the better the jerky. In general, the whiter the meat, the better it is. The angler will quickly realize that this truism rules out several species of bullhead. *Perhaps I should add that there is no such thing as a mudcat, although several species are called that—some of which, such as the bowfin, aren't even catfish. In any case, here is my list, based on common North American species. Other parts of the world, such as the Amazon Basin, produce some cats of excellent culinary quality.*

Channel Catfish from running water. (Pond-raised fish are not quite as good.) These grow to a large size, making the fillets and belly ideal for cutting into jerky strips.

Blue Catfish. These are also excellent eating and grow quite large—up to 100 pounds or better.

Flathead Catfish. Excellent eating, these large catfish are from the Mississippi River, but they have been introduced in Florida, Georgia, and no doubt other states. These prefer live food, such as hand-size bluegills, and are not scavengers. Flatheads grow to a very large size; 30- to 40-pounders are not uncommon.

White Catfish. These are excellent for the table, but they do not get as large as the channel, blue, and flathead catfish, making them harder to use for jerky. Good, though.

Farmed Catfish. These are better than no catfish at all, but the meat is usually softer than river-run fish. The fish scientists keep "improving" on these by making them grow faster. They don't necessarily taste better, however.

In any case, this recipe is for large flathead. These have a thick belly flap, rather like a slab of bacon, that is easy to slice into pieces of uniform size. I recommend ⅜- to ½-inch thickness. It's best to partly freeze the slab before slicing.

flathead strips
sea salt
Tabasco sauce

Sprinkle the strips generously with salt and lightly with Tabasco. Put the strips into a nonmetallic container and toss about to coat all sides with salt and Tabasco. Arrange on racks in a dehydrator or kitchen oven. Dry at 140°F for 6 hours or longer. For long storage (as might be the case if you jerk a 40-pound flathead), get the meat quite dry and store it in vacuum-packed bags or Mason jars.

Tsukeyaki Jerky

I make this jerky with Chef Myron's Tsukeyaki Sauce, a mixture of soy sauce, ginger, and other ingredients made especially for fish. If Myron's mix is unavailable, use any good commercial teriyaki sauce. Note that large, thick fillets can easily be cut across the grain into fingers or lengthwise into longer strips.

    2 pounds fish fillets, about ½ inch thick
    1 cup tsukeyaki or teriyaki sauce (more if needed)
    1 cup beer (more if needed)

Mix the sauce and beer in a nonmetallic container. Add the fish. If the liquid doesn't cover the fish, add some more. (Much will depend on the shape of the container.) Cover and refrigerate for 24 hours. Rig for smoking at about 150°F or so. Add some apple wood or alder wood for smoke, or use any good hardwood. Smoke for 8 hours or longer, depending on the thickness of the fillets. Cool the strips on the smoking racks, then wrap in paper towels and store in a brown bag in the refrigerator until needed.

Note: Also try this one with hard apple cider instead of beer.

Alaskan Big-Batch Fish Jerky

This recipe from Alaska works with sockeye, king, chinook, and other salmon, as well as with steelhead and other trout. Fillet the fish, leaving the skin intact. Then cut the fillets crosswise or on a diagonal into strips about ⅝ inch thick. If you prefer, cut the strips lengthwise, maintaining the same thickness. The mixture below works for 10 or 15 pounds of fillets. Double or reduce the measures as required.

    10–15 pounds trout fillets
    2 gallons boiling water
    2 cups salt
    2 cups soy sauce
    2 cups teriyaki sauce
    5 pounds brown sugar
    1 tablespoon onion powder
    1 tablespoon garlic salt
    1 tablespoon freshly ground black pepper

In a crock or other nonmetallic container of suitable size, mix all the ingredients except the fish. Stir with a wooden paddle to dissolve all the ingredients. Let the mixture cool, then mix in the fish strips. Marinate in a cool place for about 30 hours. Drain and quickly rinse the fish. Let dry to the touch in an airy place. While waiting, rig for smoking with alder or other good hardwood. Place the fish strips on racks and smoke heavily for a few hours at 140°F to 150°F. Discontinue the smoke and dry for several hours, until the jerky is dry but pliable. Store the jerky in jars or vacuum bags until needed. For long storage, dry the strips longer, until rather brittle.

Mipku

The Eskimos and Native Americans of Alaska and Canada made good use of available whale meat along the seacoasts and in Hudson Bay. (Of course, the whale is a mammal, not a fish, but it seems more fitting in this chapter.) Apparently the Native Americans can still hunt some species of whale as a source of food and fuel oil, although sport and commercial hunting is forbidden. According to *Northern Cookbook,* on which this text is based, whale meat is boneless, very dark, and fine grained. The meat is usually soaked in salt water, which is said to remove some of the blood.

To make whale jerky, called *mipku,* "Cut black whale meat into thin strips, about 8 inches wide by 2½ inches long by ½ inch thick. Hang the strips over poles to dry in the sun, or cure the strips over a driftwood fire in a log smoke house. When the meat is ready, it is hard and brittle. Break it off in small pieces and chew well. You must have strong teeth."

Jonesport Taffy

At one time, tons and tons of dried fish and salt fish, mostly cod, were shipped from New England to various parts of the world. The trade has diminished in recent years, but fish are still dried for home consumption in some coastal areas. According to James R. Babb—author, editor of Gray's Sporting Journal, *angler, and jackleg chef who lives in Maine—one of the best fish for salting is the pollack, about 18 inches long. These aren't much good for cooking fresh, and don't freeze well, he says, but, when properly dried, make the best imaginable fish chowders. Besides, he says, the local people have a good supply of pollack because the fish have a habit of nosing their way into lobster traps. If fresh cod or pollack aren't readily available, use any good lean white-fleshed fish.*

pollack or cod
salt

Split and butterfly the fish. Place a layer skin-side down in a non-metallic container. Sprinkle generously with salt. Add another layer and more salt. Repeat until all the fish are used. When a brine forms, rinse the fish and hang them on the clothesline until dry. (Take them inside in case of rain.) The dried fillets can be stored and used as needed in chowders and other recipes. For a chew of Jonesport Taffy, simply cut off a strip with a pocketknife and have at it.

PART THREE

Making Use of Jerky

These days, most jerky is consumed as a tasty snack between meals or as an energy boost on the trail. It is especially welcome as a campfire chew and as an easy-to-take, no-mess journey snack. People with very good teeth and most large family dogs simply chew it up and swallow it, but this is not the best way. For maximum flavor, simply hold the jerky in your mouth for a while without actually chewing on it. At first it is relatively tasteless, but soon the taste buds start to work and the saliva flows. After a while, the jerky will become soft enough to chew rather easily, releasing its flavor over a long period of time. Eventually it can be chewed up and swallowed, but the enjoyment should last for several minutes. That is the gustatory magic of jerky.

Although jerky has been eaten in this manner from the beginning, it was once even more important in the daily diet of the American Indians, early settlers, and other peoples the world over. It can be cooked in many soups and stews, or used in other recipes set forth in chapter 12. It can be mixed with fat and dried fruits to make pemmican, which in turn can be eaten as is or mixed with other ingredients. Jerky can even be powdered and sprinkled over other foods, or used as a soup base like bouillon cubes.

So, don't forget the old ways for camp cookery, for sea journeys, for emergency home eating, and possibly for new culinary experiences. Hunters, anglers, sustenance farmers, and survival freaks will find that making jerky and pemmican is an inexpensive way to preserve food for future use.

11

PEMMICAN

One of the greatest of the high-energy trail foods, pemmican was first made by the Native Americans. The word itself probably came from the Cree Nation, but pemmican of one kind or another was common over most of North America. It always contained powdered or ground venison or bison jerky and animal fat, and often dried fruits or berries were mixed in. The wild berries could be dried blueberries or huckleberries, cranberries, buffaloberries, and so on. Sometimes wild nuts or sunflower seeds, along with such nutritious wild edibles as powdered mesquite beans, were used in the pemmican, making it even more nutritious. Often the dried fruits and nuts were treated separately and added to the pemmican shortly before the time of consumption.

Usually, the Indians sun-dried both the jerky and the berries, and not necessarily at the same time or place. The modern practitioner, outfitted with an electric food dehydrator, will find it much easier to make relatively foolproof jerky and dried fruits. The use of seedless raisins from the supermarket as well as dried figs, blueberries, and other fruits from health food stores and trail mix outfits also simplifies the process.

These days, pemmican is usually shaped into finger foods for convenience. But convenience wasn't behind the development of pemmican. It was a means of storing food, and often relatively large slabs of pemmican were made in rawhide bags the size of a modern pillowcase. The slabs weighed 80 or 90 pounds. To make these, the Indians filled a rawhide bag with the powdered jerky, poured in melted fat, sewed the end of the bag shut—and then walked on it to mix and flatten the contents. These slabs could be stacked one atop the other for storage in large caches, sometimes underground, and, if properly made, would keep for many years. After the Europeans arrived, the Indians sold pemmican to the white trappers and settlers, as well as to the military. Each tribe made it a little differently, depending in part on what kind of game was available, and each bragged that it made the best.

Although such vegetable products as Crisco can be used more or less successfully, it's really hard to beat beef suet, because it hardens to a tallow. Sheep fat is also good, and the Indians made very good use of fat from bears, moose, caribou, buffalo, and other big game; from sea mammals such as seals and manatees; from ducks, geese, and other fowl; and from smaller animals such as opossums and armadillos. Also, bone marrow was used. Hog lard, still available in some supermarkets, is a great preservative, but it is a little too soft to be ideal for pemmican.

If you want to use animal fat and don't have big game at hand, ask your butcher for some beef suet, the best of which comes from around the kidneys. Cut the suet into ½-inch cubes. Put these into a cast-iron pot and cook on medium heat, stirring from time to time. The fat will cook out, and what's left of the cubes will float to the top. When the cubes are quite brown, they can be strained off, drained, and used as cracklings for breads and for sprinkling over salads or baked potatoes. The rendered fat should be simmered a while longer to make sure all the water is driven out, which is quite important for long storage. While still warm, rendered fat can be poured over powdered jerky, or it can be chilled and stored for later use, in which case it will have to be reheated for proper mixing with the jerky.

Most good jerky will do for making pemmican, but I think a basic recipe without all manner of spices works best. (If wanted, the spices can be added to the pemmican mix.) A dry (but not cooked) jerky cut against the grain works better simply because it is easier to reduce to a powder. Ground-meat jerky is also good. For using large batches of jerky, try cutting it into pieces with kitchen shears and then grinding it in a sausage mill or food processor. Small batches can be pounded on a heavy block of wood with a hammer. A large mortar and pestle can also be used but is not ideal. Also try a handheld grater to help reduce the jerky to small pieces, which can then be ground to a fine powder. Again, the ease of preparation depends in large part on the texture and thickness of the jerky. Anyone who wants to make a large batch of pemmican should prepare the jerky especially for grinding to a powder; that is, the meat should be cut across the grain in thin slices, then dried until it crumbles easily. I might add that powdered jerky stores well in a jar, and some people use it to season soups and stews as well as salads, sprinkling it on like salt and pepper, as discussed briefly in chapter 12. Thus, the American Eskimos powdered jerky made from moose and caribou; South Africans, ostrich and springbok; Tibetans, yak.

Most pemmican is used as a trail food or snack these days, but it can also be an ingredient for cooking a complete meal, as reflected in a few of the recipes in this chapter. (Cooking with jerky in general is covered more fully in the next chapter.)

For storage, some people shape the pemmican into fingers and wrap it in plastic wrap. Others even dip the fingers into melted paraffin, which will ensure long storage, if the pemmican has been properly made. Cakes and other shapes can be stored in airtight containers, and, of course, the modern vacuum-pack systems are ideal for storing either pemmican fingers or cakes. It should be stored in a cool place. A refrigerator is ideal.

Happy Camper Pemmican

All you need for basic pemmican is ground jerky and melted fat. Mix the melted fat into the pulverized jerky until you have a thick doughlike consistency. Add in some minced or ground dried fruit—blueberries, apricots, peaches, and so on. Shape the mixture into small loaves and wrap in cheesecloth. These loaves will keep for some time and can be taken on camping trips or journeys without refrigeration if need be. They can be eaten without cooking, giving a burst of energy, or they can be used in soups and stews.

For longer storage, wrap the loaves in cheesecloth and dip in melted paraffin. Or, better, seal the pemmican with a vacuum-pack system, if the equipment is available.

Rocky Mountain Pemmican

Here's a Rocky Mountain recipe, made with the aid of melted bone marrow. Use marrow bones from buffalo, elk, moose, caribou, or beef. To get the marrow, saw the bones off at both ends and push it out with a dowel pin. This is good stuff, and some of the Eskimos call it caribou butter.

6 cups ground jerky
4 cups dried currants, chopped
approximately ½ cup melted bone marrow
melted beeswax (optional)

Mix the jerky and currants, then add the melted marrow slowly until the mixture sticks together. Shape into small balls or cigars. Store in a cool, dry place for a few days. For longer storage and travel, dip the balls or logs into melted beeswax, or seal in plastic bags with a vacuum-pack system.

Note: Be warned that mad cow disease and similar deadly afflictions have been linked to bone marrow from cows and possibly other animals.

New England Pemmican

This jerky calls for maple sugar, but light brown sugar can also be used. The dried fruit can also be varied, depending on what's available. If you want another variation on Rocky Mountain Pemmican, for example, try dried wild buffaloberries instead of cranberries.

2 pounds jerky
1 pound beef suet or other good fat
1¼ cups maple or brown sugar
¼ pound seedless raisins
¼ pound dried cranberries

Grind the jerky in a food mill. In a nonstick loaf-shaped pan, mix the ground jerky, dried cranberries, raisins, and maple or brown sugar. Melt the fat and stir it into the mixture. Cool and remove the pemmican from the pan. Vacuum-pack in a plastic bag (or dip into melted paraffin) and store in a cool place until needed.

Honey Nut Pemmican

Honey, being a natural preservative, fits right in with the making of pemmican and can be used instead of suet or other fat. After making the pemmican, it's best to store it in the refrigerator—and do not depend on a shelf life longer than a few months. This one is closer to candy, however, than to a true pemmican. Be warned that black walnuts (most of which are harvested from the wild) are a little too strong for most tastes. For a wild mix, try ½ cup black walnuts and 2 cups hickory nuts.

4 cups powdered jerky
2½ cups seedless raisins or (better) chopped dates
2½ cups honey (approximate measure)
2½ cups chopped walnuts or other suitable nuts

In a food mill, grind the nuts and raisins or chopped dates. Mix in the powdered jerky. Gradually stir in enough honey to hold the mix together. Pour into suitable mold to a depth of ¼ inch. Chill and cut into bars. Wrap each bar in foil, or, better, seal individually in vacuum-packed bags.

Ray's Pemmican

Here's a very good recipe adapted from Internet material by Ray Audette, author of NeanderThin: A Caveman's Guide to Nutrition. *He uses beef eye of round to make the jerky, but venison or any good red meat will do. The jerky should be dry, but not cooked. (Cooking the jerky, Ray says, makes the pemmican gritty like sand.) Pound the jerky with rocks, or use a food processor.*

1 pound powdered jerky
1 pound beef suet (or ⅔ pound previously rendered tallow)
handful chopped dried cherries

Chop the suet into cubes and try it out in a cast-iron pot or large skillet. When the cracklings float to the surface, remove them and continue heating the grease to drive out all the water. Remove from the heat. When the fat is cool enough to touch (but before it turns too hard), mix it with the powdered jerky and dried cherries. Pack the mixture into cupcake forms or pie tins (or perhaps bread-stick pans) and let harden. Store in a dry place.

Note: In his book, Audette seems to favor pemmican made without dried fruit. If properly made, it will keep for a very long time—up to 100 years, he says. If dried berries are needed for a recipe, add them as needed. In other words, the pemmican will keep longer without the fruit. Also see the Caveman Jerky recipe in chapter 6.

Zuñi Candy

The sunflower might well have been the first plant cultivated by the North American Indians, and, of course, the peanut is a Native American contribution to the world's foods, as is the chili pepper. In the Southwest, cactus pear or Indian fig is a popular wild fruit, and, at one time, the honey from the repleat ant was considered a delicacy. Of course, substitutions are permitted in this recipe.

   1 cup powdered venison or beef jerky
   1 cup sunflower seeds
   1 cup chopped dried cactus pears, fruit, or berries
   ⅔ cup animal fat or Crisco
   1 tablespoon wild honey
   ½ teaspoon powdered red pepper (cayenne will do)

Mix all the ingredients and mold in a shallow baking pan. Cut into bars, wrap in plastic wrap, and store in a cool place. Nice. Like a pepper candy.

Herter's Atomic Age Pemmican and Chili con Carne

George Leonard Herter, coauthor of Bull Cook and Authentic Historical Recipes and Practices, *was somewhat haunted with fears of the atomic bomb. Many of his recipes and practices reflect this. (See also his Survival Jerky recipe on page 27.)*

2 pounds ground or powdered jerky
¼ pound ground dried fruit
¼ cup sugar
10 ounces melted suet

Mix the powdered jerky, dried fruit, and sugar, then stir in the melted suet. Form the mixture into solid blocks. Store in cans or glass jars.

Variations: Chili powder from the grocery store, Herter goes on, helps turn a cake of pemmican into a wilderness chili con carne. Simply place the pemmican into a little boiling water. Add a little chili powder to taste, along with more water if needed. Dried beans can also be added, along with plenty of water, but must be cooked for several hours. Presoaking the beans will help. Personally, I want my beans cooked separately, then put into the serving bowls as desired, along with some chopped onions and maybe some crumbled hardtack.

Sourdough's Pemmican

Here's a rather unusual recipe for a cooked pemmican. It has been adapted here from the book Cooking Alaskan, *to which it was submitted by Mrs. Aline Strutz. She says the pemmican can be eaten as is, fried like a steak, or used in a stew.*

4 cups powdered jerky
1½ cups beef suet or bear fat
¾ cup cranberry jam or wild currant jelly

½ cup soup stock (or beef stock)
½ cup brown sugar
½ cup finely ground dried blueberries, raisins, or currants
1 teaspoon minced dried wild chives
¾ teaspoon freshly ground black pepper
½ teaspoon dried savory
½ teaspoon freshly ground allspice
½ teaspoon garlic powder
½ teaspoon onion powder

Preheat the oven to 300°F. Melt the suet in a pot. Add the jelly or jam. Bring to a simmer. In a separate bowl, mix the soup stock and powdered jerky, then add the rest of the ingredients; gradually stir this mixture into the pot with the suet. Cover the pot and bake for 3½ hours. Pour a little of the mixture into a pie pan or muffin tin. If it seems too thick, add a little more stock. Then pour the mixture and let cool. Wrap each cake individually in foil. Store in a cold, dry place until needed.

12

COOKING WITH JERKY

In modern times, jerky has become popular mostly as noshing fare and trail food for hikers. Its historical use, however, was much broader, and modern practitioners can make more extensive use of it. Once the idea of reconstituting the dried meat in water is understood, the creative cook can come up with hundreds of dishes, depending in part on available ingredients and personal preference. When properly reconstituted, jerky can be used in many recipes that call for corned beef, and, sliced thinly, can be fried like bacon.

Jerky is especially useful in camp, travel trailer, and boat cookery where the use of refrigeration or bulky canned goods might be limited. Jerky is easy to pack, light in weight, and quite durable.

In any case, here are some recipes for openers, starting with an old cowboy favorite and ending with an excellent Mexican recipe to be used "the morning after."

Jowler with Saddlebag Jerky

Here's a recipe for cowboys who are tired of chewing on jerky, or who have bad teeth, or both. Any kind of good homemade jerky will work, but I like it marinated in soy sauce and cold-smoked until dry. It's best to use meat that has been cut with the grain. Any good chili pepper can be used, but a cowboy in the Southwest might well use a small wild bird pepper (so named because the birds feed on them and spread the seeds). These are very hot, so you might want to remove the seeds and inner pith. (The pith contains most of the heat.) Or try half a smoke-dried habañero if you've got one and aren't afraid of it.

    jerky
    water
    flour
    diced bird pepper (or red pepper flakes)
    salt
    rice (cooked separately)

Put the jerky, pepper, and salt in water and simmer until the jerky is reconstituted and tender. This may take 2 hours or longer, so you'll have to add a little water from time to time. When the jerky is done to your liking, remove it from the skillet. You should have about a cup of liquid left in the skillet; if not, add some water. Mix a paste with a little water and flour; stir slowly into the skillet liquid, and heat, stirring as you go, until you have a nice gravy. Put the jerky back into the skillet and simmer for a few minutes. Serve hot over rice.

Caracas

If you've got a Martha Stewart in camp, you may need a recipe with a few more ingredients than cowboy Jowler, but without beans if you're tenting. Here's an old southwestern dish that cooks easily and might fill the bill in camp or at home. It is very good, especially for brunch or perhaps a hearty breakfast.

    1½ cups chopped jerky
    1 cup chopped tomatoes

1 cup grated Monterey Jack cheese
3 chicken eggs
2 tablespoons butter
1 teaspoon salt
½–1 teaspoon cayenne pepper
½ teaspoon freshly ground cumin
toasted tortillas or toast

Freshen the jerky by soaking it in water until softened, usually overnight. Heat the butter in a skillet. Drain the jerky, then add it to the
skillet along with the tomatoes, salt, cayenne, and cumin. Cook for
a few minutes, then stir in the cheese. Whisk the eggs and stir them
in. Cook, stirring as you go, until you have a mixture not unlike
scrambled eggs. Serve hot on toasted tortillas or toast. Feeds 2 to 4.

Jerky and Garbanzo Beans

*Garbanzo beans—often called chickpeas—are widely available these days
in supermarkets and specialty shops. I have enjoyed them for many years as
a major ingredient in soup, to which they add a delightful crunch. It was not
difficult, then, for me to come up with the following recipe. It is very good,
ideal for canoe or camp cookery where the grub is light and nonperishable. I
like to top this dish with a little bottled tomato-based salsa, if I have some
at hand. If not, a little catsup or chili sauce will do.*

1 cup chopped jerky
1 cup dry garbanzo beans
red pepper flakes
salt
water
salsa (if available)

Using separate nonmetallic containers, soak the garbanzo beans and the jerky, preferably overnight. Drain them, put them into a cooking pot, and sprinkle on a few red pepper flakes and a little salt. Cover with water, bring to a boil, reduce the heat, cover tightly, and simmer for an hour, adding more water if needed. Serve hot in soup bowls, topped with a little mild, medium, or hot salsa, if available.

Zambian Stew

Central Africa makes good use of peanuts, sometimes called groundnuts, in its cuisine. Other groundnuts (such as chufas) are also used, but peanuts, imported from South America, have become standard. Ground peanuts can be used, but it's easier to use chunky peanut butter. Any good game or beef jerky can be used. The seasonings are optional, but I like some red chili pepper in mine.

1 pound jerky
1 large onion, chopped
2 tablespoons chunky peanut butter
salt (if needed)
flaked red pepper to taste (optional)
water

Soak the jerky in water for several hours and then simmer in fresh water until almost tender. Add the onion, peanut butter, salt, and red pepper flakes. Simmer for another 20 minutes. Serve hot.

Creamed Jerky

Here's a recipe that makes a wonderful (but very rich) cabin brunch or lunch on a cold winter day. It works best with a smoked jerky chopped

into a fine dice or ground coarsely in a food mill. The jerky works a little better if the strips have been cut against the grain, but chewy jerky can also be used.

1 cup minced jerky
2 cups half-and-half or light cream
¼ cup butter
¼ cup flour
salt and pepper
water

Soak the minced jerky in a little water for several hours, or simmer it for 30 minutes over very low heat, to soften it. Drain. Heat the butter in a large skillet, slowly stirring in the flour as you go. Take the skillet off the fire and stir in the half-and-half. Add the softened jerky, salt, and pepper; simmer for about 10 minutes, stirring constantly. Serve hot, spooning the mixture over toast. I also like creamed jerky served over English muffin halves, which hold lots of gravy for their size, or over sourdough biscuit halves.

New Mexico Meat Loaf

Here's a recipe from New Mexico. Use it with sun-dried beef, buffalo, or venison jerky, ground in a food mill.

1 pound red-meat jerky
1 cup raisins
1 cup sugar
1 tablespoon allspice, freshly ground
water

Soak the jerky in water overnight, then grind it in a sausage mill or chop it in a food processor. Brown the sugar in a stovetop Dutch oven or other suitable pot. Stir in 3 cups of boiling water, mixing well with a wooden spoon. Stir in the raisins, allspice, and ground meat. Put the mixture into the middle of a square of cheesecloth. Bring the ends up, forming a bag. Place a block of wood on top and drain until the liquid stops running. Slice and serve like meat loaf.

Peruvian Horse Jerky Stew

Because it is hard to find horse meat in North American markets, feel free to substitute any good red-meat jerky in this recipe. Calvin W. Schwabe's excellent book Unmentionable Cuisine, *from which this recipe has been rather freely adapted, points out that donkey meat "is more flavorful than horsemeat and is highly valued in several cuisines." Historically, however (the book goes on), the pre-Columbian version would have been made with jerked llama or guinea pig. The modern Peruvian recipe calls for calves' feet, but I have listed pig's trotters because they are more widely available in most modern supermarkets north of the border. But use calves' feet if you have them. The other meat ingredient, tripe, is also available in some supermarkets either fresh or frozen. Peruvians have a number of hot chili peppers to choose from, but most of us will have to settle for what's available in local markets and home gardens. How many you use depends on your taste and what's available. For openers, use only a few red chili peppers. If you want the stew hotter, sneak in some red pepper flakes toward the end.*

    2 pounds red-meat jerky
    2 pig's trotters, cleaned and split
    2 pounds tripe
    4–5 pounds potatoes
    2 large onions

dried red chili peppers to taste
1 cup cooking oil
1 handful fresh parsley, chopped
1 rib celery with tops, chopped
salt
chopped hard-boiled eggs (garnish)

Seed the chili peppers and soak them overnight in salted water. Bake the jerky in an oven at 350°F until browned, then simmer it in salted water until tender. In another pot, simmer the tripe and some parsley until tender. In a third pot, simmer the trotters and some chopped celery until the meat is ready to fall away from the bones. When tender, cool and chop all of the meats. Combine the pot liquors and boil gently until reduced by half.

Meanwhile, boil and mash enough potatoes to approximately equal the weight of the meats. In a stovetop Dutch oven or other suitable pot, cook the onions and chili peppers in 2 cups of water until all the water evaporates and the onions start to char. Add about 1 cup of oil and stir with a wooden spoon to keep the onions and chili peppers from sticking to the pan. Simmer for several minutes, then drain off and reserve the oil. Add all of the meats and mashed potatoes. Stir in some of the reduced stock. Cook on low until you have a thick, smooth mixture. Just before serving, stir in a little of the reserved chili oil and garnish with chopped hard-boiled eggs. Enjoy.

Bhutanese Yak Jerky Curry

Dried beef and sometimes yak, along with lamb, are favorite ingredients in the Himalayan cookery of Bhutan. The meat is cut into long thin strips about an inch wide and hung in the sun for several days. Any good red-meat jerky can be used, but note that the Bhutanese version is not salted or otherwise seasoned prior to drying. Highly seasoned jerky can be used in this recipe if necessary, but it will alter the flavor of the dish. The dish is made with lots of hot chili peppers in Bhutan, but you can adjust the heat, depending on your taste and the kind of peppers at hand. For more on Bhutanese cookery, see Indian & Chinese Cooking from the Himalayan Rim, *by Copeland Marks, the excellent work from which this recipe has been adapted.*

½ pound yak or beef jerky
½ pound string beans, split
10 dried red chili peppers (or to taste), seeded
3 cloves garlic, sliced
¼ cup peanut oil
salt to taste
water
rice (cooked separately)

Simmer the jerky in about 2 cups of water for half an hour. Add the oil, salt, chili peppers, and beans. Cover the pot and simmer for a few minutes. Stir in the garlic and cook for another half an hour, or until the jerky is tender and most of the water has cooked off. (Add more water if necessary.) Serve hot with rice.

Jerky and Rice

This recipe makes a good dish for camp cookery, partly because the ingredients are so easy to transport and store. You can even carry the jerky inside the rice container, remembering that Chinese peasants store dry sausage for long periods of time in the family rice crock.

½ pound jerky
2 cups uncooked rice

soy sauce
water

Soak the jerky overnight in water. Bring 4 cups of clean water to a boil in a pot. Add the rice. Place the jerky strips atop the rice, bring to a new boil, cover tightly, lower the heat, and simmer for 20 minutes without peeking. Remove the pot from the heat, stir in a little soy sauce to taste, and let cool for a few minutes.

Camp Stew

Here's a basic recipe that can be easily modified, depending on the vegetables you have on hand. Dried stew-beef chunks work fine, or you can cut strips of jerky with shears. Also cut the vegetables into pieces before measuring them. If you are going on a camping trip, the ingredients, except for the rice, can be measured and put into a jar or plastic bag, preferably vacuum-packed. The forager may want to add some fresh catbrier sprouts, fiddleheads, Jerusalem artichokes, and perhaps spring beauty bulbs, as available.

½ pound beef jerky chunks
1 cup dried potato pieces
1 cup dried tomato pieces
½ cup dried carrot
1 tablespoon dried bell pepper pieces
1 tablespoon dried onion bits
½ tablespoon dried garlic bits
½ tablespoon dried parsley
salt and pepper to taste
1 quart water
rice (cooked separately)

Put all the dry ingredients except the rice into a pot. Add the water and set aside for about 30 minutes. Put the pot over the heat. Bring to a boil, reduce the heat, cover tightly, and simmer for an hour or so. Serve hot over rice.

Jerky Chili

This chili can be made with any good red-meat jerky. If you use highly seasoned jerky, however, you might want to modify the ingredients accordingly.

½ pound basic jerky
¼ cup cooking oil
¼ cup prepared chili powder
1 tablespoon red pepper flakes (or to taste)
1 tablespoon dried onion flakes
1 teaspoon garlic powder
1 teaspoon cumin seeds, crushed
water
flour (if needed)

Cut the strips of jerky into ½-inch pieces. Heat the oil in a cast-iron pot. Add the jerky pieces and stir for a few minutes. Add the chili powder and stir until well mixed. Stir in the rest of the seasonings and cover well with water. Bring to a boil, reduce the heat to simmer, and cook for 3 hours, stirring from time to time and adding more water as needed. Cool the chili, then reheat it for serving. Thicken with a little paste made with flour and water, if needed. Serve hot in bowls, adding pinto beans, chopped onions, and other toppings, if wanted. Corn pone or rolled tortillas go nicely with chili, but saltines will do. Feeds 2 to 4.

Easy *Charqui* Chili

In Argentina, dried meat, made from beef, rhea, or guanaco is called charqui.
*It was, and still is, an important part of the cookery. Various stews are made
often with several different kinds of charqui, and most of them are rather
complicated. Here's an easy one, mixed to taste.*

    beef jerky, cut into small pieces
    water
    tomato paste
    chili powder
    salt

Simmer the jerky pieces in water until tender, adding more water
as needed. Stir in some tomato paste, chili powder, and salt, a little
at a time, tasting as you go. Cook until you have a thick chili. Serve
on plates, along with rice, chopped onions, and black beans. It is
permissible to mix it all together as you eat.

Jerky Bacon

Thinly sliced jerky can be fried in cooking oil and used like bacon.
I prefer to use plug jerky and slice it thinly, against the grain, just
prior to cooking. But thin strips of jerky can also be used. Use from
½ to ¾ inch of oil in a skillet, and get it quite hot. Cook the jerky
a few strips at a time until the strips are crispy. Overcooking will
give the jerky a burned taste. Drain the jerky on absorbent paper
and serve hot or warm, preferably for breakfast along with chicken
eggs and toast or perhaps grits.

Snoeksmoor

Here's an old dish from the southern part of Africa, where dried fish are an important part of the cuisine.

1 pound plain fish jerky
4 medium to large potatoes, peeled and diced
2 medium to large onions, diced
2 fresh chili peppers (jalapeños will do)
2 tablespoons cooking oil

Freshen the fish for several hours in cool water. Drain and dice. Heat the oil in a deep skillet or suitable pot, preferably cast iron. Sauté the onions until they are lightly brown. Add the potatoes and chili peppers and sauté until the potatoes are done. Add the diced fish and cook for 5 or 6 minutes on medium heat, stirring a time or two and adding a little water if needed to prevent scorching. Serve hot with rice and lots of sliced tomatoes.

Note: For better color, use 1 green chili and 1 fresh red chili, if available.

Stewed *Papa*

According to Harva Hachten's book Best of Regional African Cooking, *on which this recipe is based, dried shark is called* papa *in East Africa, and is available in Asian markets. (The coconut milk required for the recipe is also available in Asian markets, and sometimes in our supermarkets; do not use the highly sweetened piña colada mixes.) Jerky made from a shark's belly is ideal.*

½ pound shark jerky or *papa*
2 cups coconut milk

2 large tomatoes, sliced
1 large onion, sliced
1 red chili pepper, flaked
1 teaspoon curry powder
salt (if needed)
water

Bring some water to a boil in a pot. Add the shark jerky and let stand for 10 minutes. Drain the jerky and cut it into bite-size pieces, using kitchen shears. Discard the water from the pot and add the coconut milk, tomatoes, onion, curry, and chili flakes. Bring to a boil, then reduce the heat and simmer until the liquid begins to thicken and the onions are tender. Add the shark jerky and cook for about 15 minutes. Add a little salt if needed. Serve hot with a good flatbread, hardtack, or perhaps saltines.

Jerky Seasoning

Powdered or chopped jerky is used in South Africa and several other countries as a tasty and nutritious seasoning ingredient for soups and stews. In Alaska, crumbled jerky is sprinkled over scrambled eggs, salads, clam chowders, and so on. When making jerky for use as a seasoning, it's best to cut the meat thickly and across the grain so that it will be easier to crumble. The jerky pieces can be run through a food mill, or ground with a mortar and pestle. I think a plain jerky made with only salt and perhaps a little pepper works better as a seasoning than one flavored with a dozen herbs and spices.

Also see the previous chapter on making pemmican.

Caldillo de Carne Seca

Here's a good recipe from George C. Booth, author of The Food and Drink of Mexico. *Booth's version called for 2 pickled wax peppers or a drop or two of Tabasco sauce. I have substituted fresh red cayenne peppers, which add a little color as well as fire. Any hot pepper will do, used with restraint. I have also taken liberties with the amount of jerky used, reducing the measure by half.*

¼ pound jerky
1 large tomato, chopped
½ bell pepper, finely chopped
2–3 fresh red cayenne peppers, seeded and minced
1 medium onion, finely chopped
2 cloves garlic, peeled and minced
1 tablespoon cornstarch
1 teaspoon cooking oil
2½ cups water
salt and pepper
thyme

Soak the jerky in water for several hours, then chop or grind it, and drain. In a saucepan, sauté the jerky, onion, garlic, and peppers for 5 minutes. Add the tomato. Mix the cornstarch into a little of the water. Add to the pot, along with the rest of the water. Cook for 10 minutes, seasoning to taste with a little salt, pepper, and thyme. Serve hot with toasted tortillas. Feeds 4. Or 2 cowboys or newlyweds.

Note: According to Booth, this soup is a favorite with cowboys, sportsmen on the morning after, and honeymooners. "It alters the stomach, steadies the pulse, and puts new light in the eyes," he says. Enjoy.

METRIC CONVERSION TABLES

Metric U.S. Approximate Equivalents

Liquid Ingredients

Metric	U.S. Measures	Metric	U.S. Measures
1.23 ML	¼ TSP.	29.57 ML	2 TBSP.
2.36 ML	½ TSP.	44.36 ML	3 TBSP.
3.70 ML	¾ TSP.	59.15 ML	¼ CUP
4.93 ML	1 TSP.	118.30 ML	½ CUP
6.16 ML	1¼ TSP.	236.59 ML	1 CUP
7.39 ML	1½ TSP.	473.18 ML	2 CUPS OR 1 PT.
8.63 ML	1¾ TSP.	709.77 ML	3 CUPS
9.86 ML	2 TSP.	946.36 ML	4 CUPS OR 1 QT.
14.79 ML	1 TBSP.	3.79 L	4 QTS. OR 1 GAL.

Dry Ingredients

Metric	U.S. Measures	Metric		U.S. Measures
2 (1.8) G	1⁄16 OZ.	80 G		2⅘ OZ.
3½ (3.5) G	⅛ OZ.	85 (84.9) G		3 OZ.
7 (7.1) G	¼ OZ.	100 G		3½ OZ.
15 (14.2) G	½ OZ.	115 (113.2) G		4 OZ.
21 (21.3) G	¾ OZ.	125 G		4½ OZ.
25 G	⅞ OZ.	150 G		5¼ OZ.
30 (28.3) G	1 OZ.	250 G		8⅞ OZ.
50 G	1¾ OZ.	454 G	1 LB.	16 OZ.
60 (56.6) G	2 OZ.	500 G	1 LIVRE	17⅗ OZ.

Appendix A

Jerky Ingredients and Safety

At its Web site, the U.S. Department of Agriculture (USDA) recommends that jerky meat be heated to 160°F before drying. In other words, the meat should be fully cooked—and well done at that!—before the home drying process starts. Some of the studies cited were of ground meat, dried both with and without the help of salt. Well, hell, anyone who makes jerky from USDA-inspected ground meat and no salt is really asking for trouble. Under the jurisdiction of this agency, the nation's ground meat and mass-produced chickens have come to a very sorry state and are considered toxic substances these days.

I, for one, don't want my jerky cooked, for the same reason that I don't want a T-bone steak cooked over 140°F. Nor is it necessary if you have good meat. Of course, there is a small risk in eating anything, including grapes and apples, but beef has been eaten raw for centuries in such dishes as steak tartare. Adding salt to the meat and removing the moisture in the drying process also inhibits bacterial growth, making the meat even safer.

What to do? There is no easy answer. Personally, I'll continue to use wild game and carefully selected supermarket beef to make jerky the way it ought to be made—at a low temperature for a long period of time—but I will not use market-ground meat, chicken, commercial turkey, or pork. My best advice, set forth in the chapter on beef, is to buy large chunks of meat from a local source of range-fed animals or to hunt and butcher your own venison. If you buy from a meat market, do so carefully; choose large cuts of meat with a long expiration date and a bright, fresh color. Remember that the more the meat is handled before it is packaged, the more likely it is to be contaminated.

Much of the considerable problem with modern meats is caused by bunching the animals or birds into close quarters, feeding them man-made food that includes animal blood and parts from the slaughterhouse, and then processing them in large numbers. It's somewhat like the bad apple that spoiled the whole barrel. In any case, the proper feed for cattle is grass, with a little whole grain, if they are lucky. The same statement can be made for pen-raised caribou or elk.

The bottom line: I will eat jerky made by any of the recipes and techniques in this book, if I know that the meat was good to start with and if the jerky was properly made, preferably with plenty of salt. For the other side of the story, however, check out the USDA's alerts at its Web site (www.fsis.usda.gov) or call (800) 535-4555.

Meanwhile, here's my take on a few ingredients commonly used in jerky.

Ac'cent. See monosodium glutamate.

brine. Very salty water used to cure or marinate meats. Salt and water (which should be pure) are the main ingredients, although various herbs and spices can be added, and often some additive such as saltpeter is included to help preserve the meat and retain its color.

cold-smoking. Smoking meats and other foods at a low temperature for a long period of time. The meat is not cooked during the process, and, if possible, the temperature is held below 100°F. The process can be used for making jerky, or possibly as a step in making jerky.

cure. A dry mixture or a brine containing salt or curing salts such as sodium nitrate. Most mixes contain spices and herbs, and some contain sugar or other sweetener.

curing salt. This mix is ordinary salt with a small amount of sodium nitrate, saltpeter, or some such compound mixed in.

dry cure. A mix of common salt and other preservatives, such as sodium nitrate or saltpeter. It is rubbed onto the meat instead of being used in a brine. Most dry cures contain spices and herbs, and some contain sugar or other sweeteners. Note that meat salted down in a waterproof container with a cure or with ordinary salt will form its own brine.

hot-smoking. Flavoring meats or other foods with the aid of smoke during the cooking process. Most hot-smokers will attain a temperature of 200°F or higher. The process is not used extensively in jerky making. *See* cold-smoking.

Liquid Smoke. A liquid ingredient, readily available in supermarkets, that has been flavored by smoke. It's available in hickory and other flavors. Some practitioners consider it safer than real smoke because the tar, resin, and soot are removed in the manufacturing process. It may have some value as a meat preservative. In any case, use this stuff carefully and in small amounts lest you overpower the good flavor of the meat.

monosodium glutamate (MSG). A crystalline salt that enhances the flavor of meat and other food, popular in some Asian cuisines. It had a flurry of popularity in the United States, then dropped out of the culinary picture when it was deemed unsafe to eat. It does, however, remain as an ingredient in many old recipes. A little from time to time won't hurt anything, except possibly for people who are allergic to the stuff. Also called MSG, it is a major ingredient in Ac'cent.

pickling salt. A refined salt that contains no iodine. It is used in pickling, canning, and meat curing. It can be used for making jerky, but ordinary salt will do.

potassium nitrate. See saltpeter.

salt. Sodium chloride. Ordinary table salt is quite inexpensive and works fine for jerky. This is usually salt that has been mined and refined, robbing it of some of its minerals. Sea salt usually contains more minerals and has more flavor, but it is far more expensive than regular table salt. Some practitioners recommend that iodized salt be avoided, but I like it. Suit yourself.

saltpeter. Potassium nitrate, NO_3, a naturally occurring mineral that was once used in meat curing and the manufacture of gunpowder. Today it is banned for commercial meat-curing use, having been replaced by sodium nitrate and sodium nitrite, both used in limited quantities. Saltpeter is, however, safe to use in small amounts—but I wouldn't want to eat it every day. Many of the old-time recipes for cured meats and sausage call for saltpeter, and some of the recipes in this book reflect this practice. It can, however, be omitted in recipes that call for lots of ordinary salt. Although saltpeter is a meat preservative, its main purpose is to help retain a reddish color in the meat. I once thought that the sale of saltpeter had been banned, or highly restricted, but while working on this book I purchased a bottle off the shelf in my local pharmacy.

seasoning salt. Regular salt flavored with herbs, spices, and other ingredients. Several kinds are available in spice departments at supermarkets, such as lemon-pepper and hickory-smoked.

smoking. See cold-smoking and hot-smoking.

sodium nitrate. A sodium salt that is used in meat curing as well as in fertilizers and explosives. It is toxic and should be used in small amounts, usually thoroughly mixed with ordinary salt. Although some experts, some of whom sell curing mixes, say it is necessary in meat curing, its use is primarily to preserve color in sausage, corned beef, and so on.

sodium nitrite. A compound used in curing meats. It is toxic and should be used in small amounts. *See* sodium nitrate.

soy sauce. A wonderful Chinese condiment and standard ingredient made with soy, salt, barley, and other ingredients. Low-salt or "lite" soy sauces are marketed, but these are not recommended for jerky unless the recipe also calls for salt. Note, however, that a "light" soy sauce refers to the color and may indeed contain more salt than "dark."

Appendix B

Sources

Jerky seasoning mixes are now available in supermarkets and electric dehydrators are being sold in large discount stores. Most towns have a meat shop in addition to regular supermarkets, making it easy to get custom meats. Some of the best beef for making jerky is range fed. Check into buying a steer from a local farmer and having it butchered to your specifications.

Meats and ingredients for making jerky are also available by mail order and over the Internet these days. Here are a few of the sources of meats, seasonings, and equipment for making jerky.

Allied Kenco Sales, 26 Lyerly Street, Houston, TX 77022. Jerky-making equipment, spices, cures, and supplies. Telephone: (800) 356-5189.

Billabong Jerky. Outback jerky of several sorts, including emu, kangaroo, and crocodile. The early Aussie cowboys were especially fond of beef jerky—and still are. Web site: www.jerky.com.au.

Chef's, 5073 Centennial Boulevard, Colorado Springs, CO 80919. Kitchen equipment and aids, including dehydrators, meat grinders, vacuum-pack systems. Telephone: (800) 338-3232. Web site: www. chefscatalog.com.

Cumberland General Store, P.O. Box 4468, Alpharetta, GA 30023. This mail-order firm publishes an interesting catalog, chock-full of hard-to-find old-time items, spices, cures, and seasonings.

Decosonic, Inc., 2159 South Tamiami Trail, Venice, FL 32493. These people market a vacuum-seal system using either heat-sealed plastic bags or Mason jars.

Eldon's Sausage and Jerky Supply Catalog, HC 75, Box 113A2, Kooskia, ID 83539. Jerky seasonings, equipment, jerky guns, meat grinders, dehydrators, smokers, and so on. Telephone: (800) 926-4949. Web site: www.eldonsausage.com.

Excalibur, 6083 Power Inn Road, Sacramento, CA 95824. Excalibur brand dehydrators and accessories. These have square trays, up to nine, depending on the model. Telephone: (800) 875-4254.

Grandma LaMure's Spice 'n Slice, P.O. Box 26061, Phoenix, AZ 85068. Convenient small-batch seasoning mixes for sausage and jerky.

L.E.M. Products, Inc., Jerky and sausage seasonings, curing salts, and spices, as well as dehydrators, jerky shooters, and vacuum-pack systems. Telephone: (877) 536-7763. Web site: www.lemproducts.com. E-mail: info@lemproducts.com.

Magic Mill, P.O. Box 7, Hampton, NE 68843. This firm makes the Magic Aire dehydrator, featuring trays that are basically rectangular with rounded corners. The trays are stackable, up to six high.

Myron's Fine Foods, 1 River Street, Millers Falls, MA 01349. Myron's 20-Gauge, a wild-game and fish sauce, and other fine sauces. Telephone: (978) 544-2820. Web site: www.chefmyrons.com.

Nationalwide Marketing, Inc., 340 Townsend Street, San Francisco, CA 94107. Foodsavor vacuum-pack systems for plastic bags and Mason jars. Great for jerky and pemmican.

Nesco American Harvest, P.O. Box 237, Two Rivers, WI 54241. This firm manufactures several round dehydrators with stackable trays—up to twelve—along with jerky guns and other accessories. Telephone: (800) 288-4545.

Pendery's, 1221 Manufacturing Street, Dallas, TX 75207. Spices, spice mixes for jerky and sausage, chili peppers, Mexican food supplies and equipment, cookbooks, and other items. Telephone: (800) 533-1870. Web site: www.penderys.com.

Penzey's, Ltd., P.O. Box 1448, Waukesha, WI 53187. Spices, spice mixes, and seasonings.

Professional Marketing Group, Inc., 16817 188th Avenue SE, Renton, WA 98058. This firm markets the PressAIREizer dehydrators, along with a jerky press, mesh screens, spices, and so on. The unit features round trays in which the air is said to move up an outside ring and flow horizontally across each tray. Stackable to a whopping thirty-five trays. Telephone: (800) 227-3769.

Ronco Innovation, Inc., P.O. Box 1879, Van Nuys, CA 91406. This outfit markets a dehydrator with round trays, expandable to five. The air flows upward by convection, without a fan.

The Sausage Maker, 1500 Clinton Street, Building 123, Buffalo, NY 14206. Jerky seasonings, dehydrators, vacuum-pack systems, smokers, meat grinders, and other meat-curing items. Telephone: (888) 490-8525. Web site: www.sausagemaker.com.

Waring, 3495A Lawson Boulevard, Oceanside, NY 11572. Waring makes a circular dehydrator with clear trays, giving a good view of the contents during the drying process. Telephone: (203) 379-0731.

Index

139

About the Author

A. D. Livingston claims to have hop-scotched through life. Navy at seventeen. Mechanical engineering at Auburn. Atomic bombs at Oak Ridge. Creative writing at University of Alabama. Missiles and rockets at Huntsville. Published a novel and played a little poker. Travel editor at *Southern Living* magazine. Freelance writing and outdoor photography. Word man for fishing rods and bait-casting reels with Lew Childre, the genius of modern fishing tackle. Bought the family farm. Lost the back forty publishing *Bass Fishing News*. Lost the rest of the farm manufacturing fishing lures. Back to freelancing. Published twenty-something books. For the past sixteen years—the sweetest of all, he claims—he has been the food columnist for *Gray's Sporting Journal*. What in his previous work experience qualifies him for this position? Nothing whatsoever. He hates to work, but all his life he has loved to hunt and fish and to cook and eat the bounty. And he loves to write about it his way.